FELT SO GOOD

Published by Sellers Publishing, Inc.

161 John Roberts Road, South Portland, Maine 04106
Visit our Web site: www.sellerspublishing.com
E-mail: rsp@rsvp.com

English translation copyright © 2014 Sellers Publishing, Inc.
All rights reserved.

Edited by Robin Haywood.
Translated from Norwegian by Margaret Berge Hartge.

First published in 2005 as
Bare ULL by Tone Rørseth
copyright 2005 © Cappelen Damm AS

ISBN 13: 978-1-4162-4527-8
Library of Congress Control Number: 2014931410

10 9 8 7 6 5 4 3 2 1

Printed and bound in China.

FELT SO GOOD

70+ FELTED AND PLAIN WOOL DESIGNS FOR YOU AND YOUR HOME

BY TONE RØRSETH

SELLERS
PUBLISHING

contents

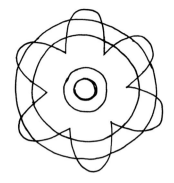

foreword

I first discovered the joys of working with wool about six years ago when my son started kindergarten at a creative Waldorf School.

Some of the kindergarteners' parents met once a week to felt together. I also joined the group and became completely enamored with the materials we used: wool roving, merino wool, and ready-made wool felt.

Since then, I have created many small and large projects, and I have stored many more ideas to memory. This book is an opportunity for me to share some of these ideas and to show you all the wonderful and fun things that you can make from wool!

I hope that this book illustrates the great variety of things that can be made from this wonderful fabric. The creations are both fun and practical with objects for both your home and your wardrobe.

Most of the projects are very simple to make and can be finished in an evening or a weekend. Anyone can make them. You only need a little enthusiasm and imagination. No education in crafts is necessary.

In this book you will find a large variety of projects including decorative hairpins, fun pillows, and even baggage tags for your suitcases. You may simply copy these projects or modify them to your own style and taste. Most important is that you are satisfied with the results and enjoy the process of making your projects.

I hope that this book will inspire you with many new ideas, and help to kick-start your own creativity.

Happy crafting,

Materials

Wool Roving
This wool works well for needle felting and wet felting. It is soft and easy to work with. Lamb's wool from Nepal has a natural, coarse feel.

Nepal Wool Felt
These are hand-felted wool sheets, about ³⁄₁₆ inch (5 mm) thick. The sheets can be bought in smaller pieces, about 12 x 10 inches (30 x 25 cm) each. There are different qualities available, from a soft feel to a stiffer, coarser texture. These sheets can be used to make small purses, decorations, figures, etc.

Wool Felt by the Yard
This felt is sold by the yard and comes in different widths. It is typically a blend of 80 percent wool and 20 percent polyester, and it is about ³⁄₃₂ inch (3 mm) thick. This felt works well for making mittens, slippers, and purses.

Hobby Felt
This felt comes in different sizes, typically consists of 30 percent wool and 70 percent viscose, and is about ¹⁄₃₂ inch (1 mm) thick. It does not fray.

Crafting Felt
This felt is made of 100 percent polyester, is ³⁄₁₆ inch (5 mm) thick, and has a coarse texture.

Tools
Needles for felting (different gauges include regular, medium, and fine), felting mats, sewing needle, thread, sharp textile scissors, small embroidery scissors, darning needle, pins, measuring tape, soap and water, textile glue, hobby glue, crochet needle, parchment paper, tracing paper, textile pen, embroidery floss, and wool yarn.

Techniques

Needle Felting
You will need a felting needle, wool roving, and a felting mat or some thick, soft padding that can protect the tip of the needle. By repeatedly stabbing the sharp needle through the wool roving, the wool fibers will start to interweave and become more compact. In this way you can create small or large items and details in 3-D. The wool will shrink in size as it increasingly becomes more compact. The needle is very sharp, so it is best to store it in a container when not in use. Always work the needle straight up and down, it will break very easily if you use it at an angle. The thinnest needle works best for very thin and small details, while the largest needle is used for larger pieces. You will use the medium sized needle the most.

Wet Felting
Wet felting gives you a strong and lasting product. Start by first dipping the wool roving in warm soapy water. Then manipulate the wet wool with your hands, kneading and rolling the wool. Keep working the wool while you alternately dip the roving into cold and warm water. You can make nice balls, figures, and flat pieces of different sizes depending how many layers of wool you use.

I have used ready-made wool felt bought by the yard, or thicker felt sold in smaller pieces for most of these projects. It is so simple. You can cut felt into any shape and you do not have to worry about the material fraying. Then sew the pieces together and make whatever you want.

Felting Wool
Felting wool clothing in the washing machine is a good way to recycle old items. Clothes you no longer use get a new life and function. Wash the wool at 100-140 degrees F (40-60 degrees C), or on the hot setting of a washing machine, and you will get a material that is naturally warm and insulating, strong and stable, soft and water resistant . . . a fabric with so many fabulous qualities! You start with a wool garment and end up with felt! In the process, you have helped the environment by recycling.

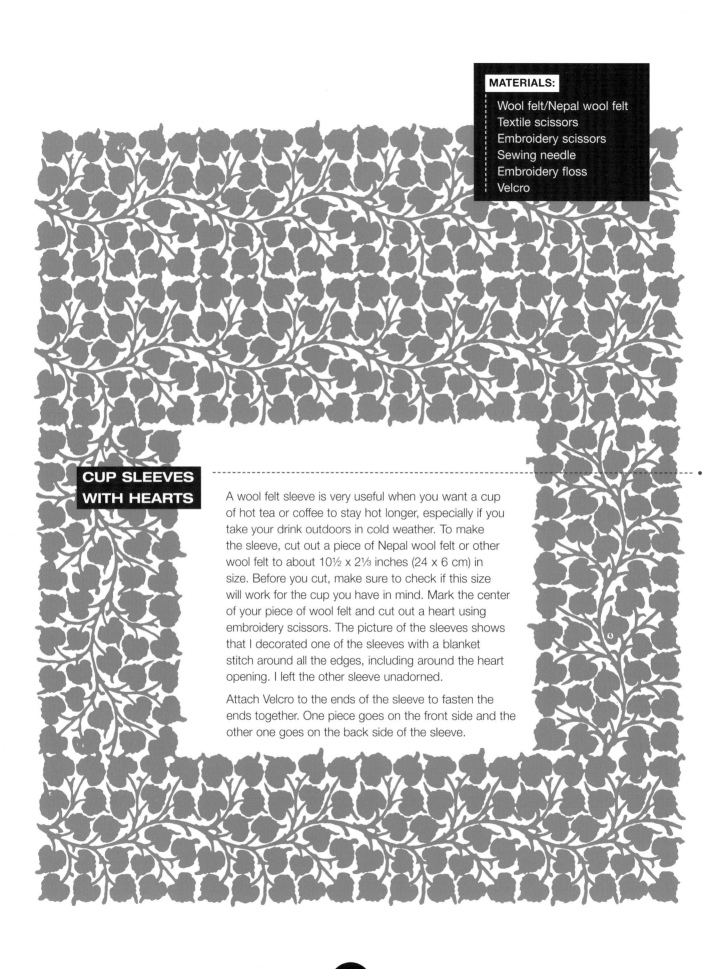

MATERIALS:

Wool felt/Nepal wool felt
Textile scissors
Embroidery scissors
Sewing needle
Embroidery floss
Velcro

CUP SLEEVES WITH HEARTS

A wool felt sleeve is very useful when you want a cup of hot tea or coffee to stay hot longer, especially if you take your drink outdoors in cold weather. To make the sleeve, cut out a piece of Nepal wool felt or other wool felt to about 10½ x 2⅓ inches (24 x 6 cm) in size. Before you cut, make sure to check if this size will work for the cup you have in mind. Mark the center of your piece of wool felt and cut out a heart using embroidery scissors. The picture of the sleeves shows that I decorated one of the sleeves with a blanket stitch around all the edges, including around the heart opening. I left the other sleeve unadorned.

Attach Velcro to the ends of the sleeve to fasten the ends together. One piece goes on the front side and the other one goes on the back side of the sleeve.

MATERIALS:

- Wool felt
- Textile scissors
- Velcro
- Tracing paper
- Pen
- Embroidery scissors
- Embroidery floss
- Sewing needle
- Textile glue

THERMOS SLEEVES WITH CUTE ANIMALS

patterns are 100%

A felt sleeve decorated with whimsical animal motifs is a fun addition to any thermos bottle. Start by cutting out a piece of wool felt measuring about 4 x 10 inches (10 x 25 cm), making sure that the size will fit around your thermos.

Attach two Velcro pieces at each end of the wool felt where the ends will overlap when the sleeve is on your thermos. You will end up with two Velcro pieces for the front and two for the back of the wool felt. Make a pattern in the shape an animal face or trace one of the patterns in this book. Transfer your pattern onto the wool felt using tracing paper. It is best to use embroidery scissors to cut out the animal faces or other intricate images with fine details.

Attach the faces by sewing them onto the wool felt using small basting stitches. You can also attach the images using textile glue. Place the sleeve under a heavy box after you have finished decorating it until the glue dries. Sew around the edges of the sleeve using blanket stitches to finish it off.

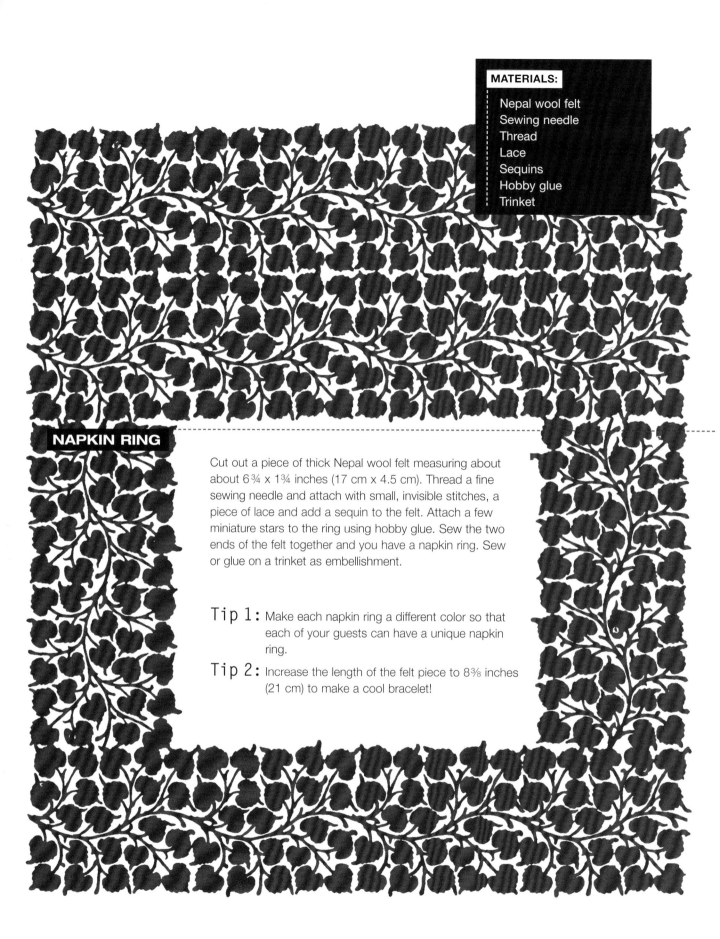

MATERIALS:

Nepal wool felt
Sewing needle
Thread
Lace
Sequins
Hobby glue
Trinket

NAPKIN RING

Cut out a piece of thick Nepal wool felt measuring about about 6¾ x 1¾ inches (17 cm x 4.5 cm). Thread a fine sewing needle and attach with small, invisible stitches, a piece of lace and add a sequin to the felt. Attach a few miniature stars to the ring using hobby glue. Sew the two ends of the felt together and you have a napkin ring. Sew or glue on a trinket as embellishment.

Tip 1: Make each napkin ring a different color so that each of your guests can have a unique napkin ring.

Tip 2: Increase the length of the felt piece to 8⅜ inches (21 cm) to make a cool bracelet!

HOT WATER BOTTLE COVER

Wouldn't these hot water bottle covers make wonderful gifts for friends who live in cold places?

To make one, you can use wool felt or a felted wool sweater, as shown in the pictures. (Follow instructions for felting a wool garment on page 7.) Place a hot water bottle on some tracing paper and draw around the bottle (or use pattern 13A on page 129).

Cut out one piece of felt for the front of the bottle and one piece for the back. The neckline on the front of a sweater can be used for the front of the bottle and the back neckline of the same sweater can be used for the back.

Embroider letters using a cross stitch to embellish the front of the cover. See pattern 13 on page 129.

Slip a felting mat or a sheet of Styrofoam under the front piece of the hot water bottle cover and felt buttons, bows, pearls, etc., onto the cover.

Place the two cut-out felt pieces on top of each other. Make sure that the right sides are out on both the front and the back of the cover. Stitch around the edges using a blanket stitch. Be careful to leave an opening large enough for the hot water bottle to be inserted through the bottom of the cover. Cut out a buttonhole in the little flap at the bottom of the cover, and stitch around it using a blanket stitch. Attach a nice button on the back side of the cover so you can close the opening by buttoning the flap.

Use a clean can, and measure the can's circumference and height. Calculate how many rows of wool felt strips measuring ¾ inch (2 cm) wide will be needed to cover the height of the can and how many rows are needed for the circumference. Cut out all the wool felt strips you will need. Place one strip that is the length of the circumference horizontally. This will be the bottom piece. Sew all the vertical strips to the bottom horizontal strip alternating the placement of the vertical strips on the front and in back of the horizontal strip. You have now completed the first row. Take a horizontal strip and weave it in, alternating between the front and back of the vertical strips. You have now completed the second row. Repeat this step until you have woven all the pieces together, and have a woven mat of the right size to cover your can. When you are finished weaving, hand sew the strip ends together on all the sides using color matching thread. Then you can hand stitch the sides together and cover your can with your woven tube.

You may want to make several felt covers of the same color or play with matching hues. These woven containers are great for storing pens, brushes, or any other small objects you may want to store upright.

MATERIALS:

Cans
Ruler
Wool felt
Textile scissors
Sewing needle
Thread

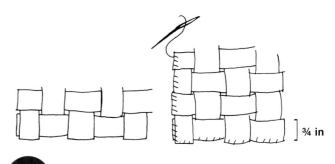

¾ in

EGG CUPS

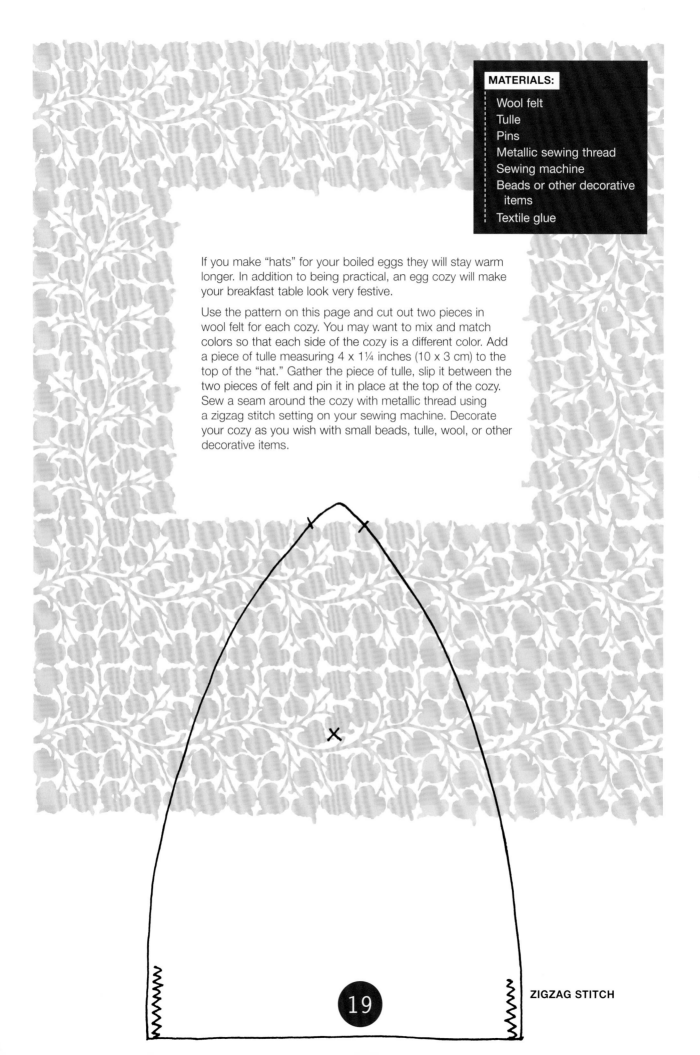

If you make "hats" for your boiled eggs they will stay warm longer. In addition to being practical, an egg cozy will make your breakfast table look very festive.

Use the pattern on this page and cut out two pieces in wool felt for each cozy. You may want to mix and match colors so that each side of the cozy is a different color. Add a piece of tulle measuring 4 x 1¼ inches (10 x 3 cm) to the top of the "hat." Gather the piece of tulle, slip it between the two pieces of felt and pin it in place at the top of the cozy. Sew a seam around the cozy with metallic thread using a zigzag stitch setting on your sewing machine. Decorate your cozy as you wish with small beads, tulle, wool, or other decorative items.

ZIGZAG STITCH

MATERIALS:

Wool roving
Felting needle
Felting mat
Embroidery floss
Sewing needle
Metal wire, 15¾ inches
  (40 cm) long
Darning needle
Hobby glue

SIMPLY ADORABLE OWLS

These adorable owls are made from wool roving. To start, take a piece of soft wool roving and shape it into a ball using your hands. Take another thin piece of roving and wrap it around the ball shape. Use a felting needle (see page 7) and repeatedly stab the ball to make it more compact. Repeat the process. If you want to create a multi-colored owl, apply several thin layers of colored roving and felt them onto the ball. Work your needle around the ball to get a smooth exterior and a correct shape. You can decide if you want a softer, fluffier owl or a smaller, more evenly textured and compact owl. The owl's texture and size is determined by how much you work the wool roving with your felting needle.

Place a small piece of roving on the felting mat and felt it into a small ear. Repeat for the owl's other ear. Felt or glue the ears to the body. Attach small, differently colored roving pieces for the eyes and the beak by felting them onto the bird. Use embroidery floss and sew back stitches around the owl's eyes and beak. This will enhance the outline of the eyes and beak.

Make the owl's feet by using an about 8 inches (20 cm) long metal wire. Poke holes with a darning needle at the bottom of the owl for the feet. Dip the leg ends of the metal feet into a little glue before you insert them into the owl.

Tip: Attach a string to the middle of the owl's head and you can hang it up.

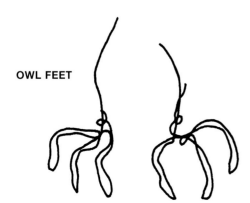

OWL FEET

20

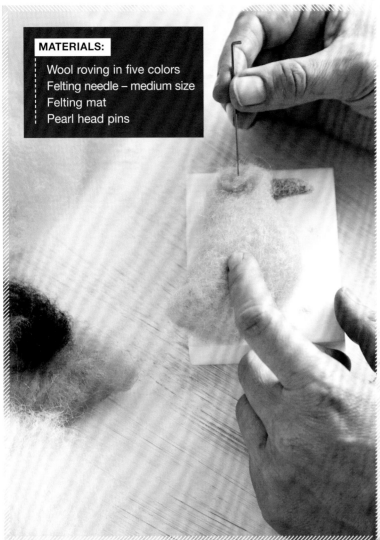

MATERIALS:

Wool roving in five colors
Felting needle – medium size
Felting mat
Pearl head pins

BIRD PINCUSHION

Create a decorative, practical wool felt pincushion
for the safekeeping of your pins and needles.

To start, take a large piece of roving and shape it
into a bird by repeatedly stabbing the roving with
a medium-sized felting needle (see page 7). Keep
adjusting the shape as you work. Use a felting mat
under your work.

Work the bird's head and body into one solid shape.
Place a small piece of turquoise roving on the felting
mat and felt it into a stiff beak. Place the beak on the
bird and attach it by felting it onto the bird's head.
Felt onto the bird small yellow, white, and black roving
pieces for the eyes. Shape a small, flat area on the bird's
underside so that the bird will sit well on a flat surface.
Add four pins as legs for additional stability. Now you
have created a four-legged bird!

22

HAPPY
BIRDS
MOBILE

MATERIALS:

Tracing paper
Pen
Hobby felt/wool felt
Small, sharp scissors
Sewing needle
Embroidery floss
Wool roving
Tulle
Cotton thread
Feathers
Sequins
Fishing line
Branch

This project features many colorful, happy felt birds. To make this mobile, start with the bird patterns you see on this page and transfer them onto felt with the help of tracing paper. Cut out two birds in wool felt from the same pattern. Sew the pieces together with embroidery floss, leaving a small opening. Stuff the bird with some wool roving to give it a 3-D effect. Add a little piece of tulle for the tail. You may want to add small pieces of felt for the bird's eyes, and wool roving, embroidery, or a little felt heart as embellishment.

Thread three finished birds along with some sequins onto a strong cotton thread. Tie 5–6 threads with happy birds onto a branch and hang it up with a length of fishing line.

patterns are 100%

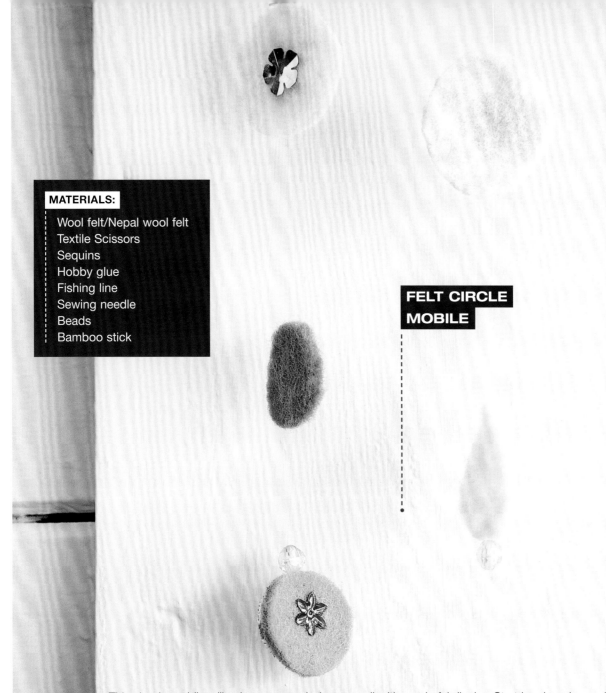

MATERIALS:

Wool felt/Nepal wool felt
Textile Scissors
Sequins
Hobby glue
Fishing line
Sewing needle
Beads
Bamboo stick

FELT CIRCLE MOBILE

This simple mobile will enhance any window or wall with a colorful display. Start by choosing a pleasing color combination of felt pieces from your stash, and cut out circles with a diameter of about 1⅜ inches (3.5 cm). Place 7–8 circles in a row on the floor and rearrange the circles until you get a pretty sequence of colors. Decorate some of the circles by gluing on sequins.

Use a sewing needle to thread the circles onto a fishing line. Make sure to tie a knot in the fishing line before you start. To add beads to the line, make a knot on the line in front of and after each bead, and the beads will stay in place when you hang the mobile.

Tie all the decorated fishing lines to a bamboo stick. Use a simple knot to tie the lines to the stick so you can easily remove them later if you wish.

To store your mobile when it is not in use, wrap each line individually around a long and narrow piece of cardboard (or a folded 8½ x 11 sheet of heavy weight paper) and fasten the ends with tape.

MATERIALS:

Twigs with acorns, about 20
Thin, soft metal wire
Wool roving
Soapy water or felting needle
Felting mat
Glue gun
Hobby glue

It is easy to find twigs with acorn caps attached lying on the ground in the fall. You may want gather pick a few to create this charming acorn heart. Start by wrapping a thin metal wire around each twig and tying them together. Alternate the acorn caps directions, placing one to the left, the next to the right, and so on. Use the acorn twig garland to make a heart and fasten the ends of the garland together at the bottom point of the heart. Adjust the heart shape as needed. The acorn caps are delicately attached to the twig. If any of the acorn shells fall off as you work, just reattach them with a glue gun when you have finished making the heart.

You are now ready to make new, colorful, felted acorns for the empty caps. Pick a color of wool roving and take a very small piece. Roll it into a ball, dip the ball into soapy water, roll it some more, dip it into clear water, and then roll again. Repeat until the ball is firm. Let the balls dry completely after you have finished making them. You can glue the felted balls to the acorn caps after they have dried.

You can also make the felted balls using a felting needle if you prefer this method. Roll a piece of wool roving in your hands, place it on a felting mat, and stab it repeatedly with a felting needle until it becomes a compact ball. Make sure to use a felting mat whenever you are working with a felting needle. Tie a ribbon or a string to the heart and hang it up.

You can make your own round wool felt pictures by using traditional embroidery hoops. Fasten wool felt between the hoops, tighten and cut away any excess material. Create your own picture series using felted motifs, embroidery, cut-out wool felt images, buttons, and decorative pins. The possibilities are endless.

To make the crows, see pattern 5 on page 135. Trace the crows onto tracing paper and transfer the images to the felt stretched on the embroidery hoop. Use small pieces of black wool roving and a medium to fine felting needle to create the crow silhouettes. Don't forget to put a felting mat under your work. Keep adding pieces of roving until you achieve the desired bird shape. You can choose if you want your picture to be flat and dense, or more textured by leaving some roving "loose." The more you work the roving into the background, the denser the result will be.

You can create words with roving to enhance an image, or just use words by themselves as image. Make a word pattern on a tracing paper, transfer it onto the wool felt background, and felt the words using wool roving and a felting needle.

If you want to embroider letters using cross stitches and/or hearts using backstitches, see pattern 5 on page 132.

EMBROIDERY HOOP ART

MATERIALS:
Tracing paper
Pen
Embroidery hoops
Wool felt/ hobby felt
Wool roving
Felting needle
Felting mat
Sewing needle
Embroidery floss
Button

MATERIALS:

Wool felt/hobby felt
Double-sided tape
Wool yarn
Sewing needle
Wool roving
Soapy water
Darning needle

You can wrap gifts in wool felt, hobby felt, or felted wool garments for a unique look. Just use the same techniques as when you wrap your gifts in paper. Place the box sideways on the felt and bring the sides together. Fold in three flaps on the underside of the box and cut away excess felt. Fasten the felt with double-sided tape or sew a simple seam at the side and under the package. Your felt wrapping material will need to extend 8–10 inches (20–25 cm) above the box to tie a simple knot at the top of the package. Cut the wrapping as necessary to make flaps long enough to tie together. After you have made your knot, cut the ends to shape them.

Attach a string of yarn threaded with wool balls to the package to embellish it. Make the wool balls by felting roving using the wet felting method (see page 7). Use a darning needle to attach the wool balls to the yarn by threading them through the center. A yarn string with felted wool balls also makes an attractive embellishment for a bottle.

FELTED GIFT WRAPPING

31

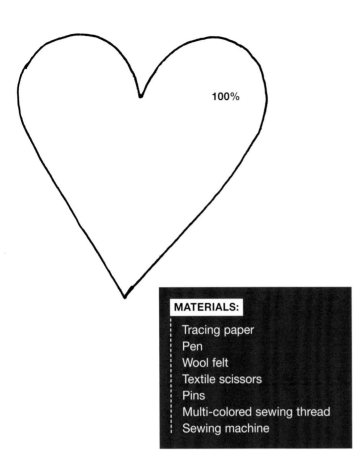

100%

TIC TAC TOE!

Make your own tic-tac-toe game pieces using wool felt.

First cut out two hearts and two Xs for each piece. Place two pieces of the same kind on top of each other, pin, and then sew them together on a sewing machine using the zigzag stitch setting. Use a multi-colored sewing thread if you want a colorful effect. You could also do a blanket stitch around each piece for a different look. Make all the pieces in the same way. You will need three hearts and three Xs to play the game. Then you can start to play.

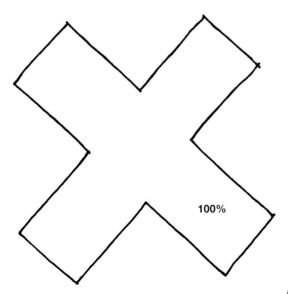

100%

all puzzle pieces are 90%;
enlarge to 110%

PUZZLE
PIECE COASTERS

Make coasters that look like puzzle pieces for a playful look. You can use the patterns on this page. Use Nepal wool felt for the bottom of the coaster and thin hobby felt for the top.

Sharp textile scissors are a must for cutting out the pieces so that the coaster's edges will be even. Glue the two felt pieces for each coaster together with textile glue and place the coasters under heavy books until the glue has dried. You may want to trim the edges, if needed, after the coasters have dried. Use the small puzzle pieces under glasses and the largest puzzle piece under a pitcher.

MATERIALS:

Nepal wool felt
Hobby felt/wool felt
Textile scissors
Textile glue

FELT ENVELOPE

Surprise your sweetheart or a friend with an envelope full of wool hearts!

This gift would be appropriate for birthdays, Valentine's Day, or for any ordinary day when someone you know needs a little encouragement.

Use hobby felt for this project because the material is easy to fold into an envelope shape. Set your iron on low for pressing the folds. Use pattern 2 on page 122. Trace the pattern on tracing paper, transfer it to the felt, and cut it out.

First fold the side flaps in towards the middle, and then fold up the bottom flap. Iron lightly. Fasten the flaps in place with pins and sew only the flaps together using basting stitches. You may also want to decorate the envelope with basting stitches. Cut out hearts from wool felt and put them in the envelope — and why not add one or two movie tickets?

Finish by sewing a decorative button onto the outside of the closing flap.

MATERIALS:

- Tracing paper
- Pen
- Hobby felt
- Textile scissors
- Iron
- Pins
- Sewing needle
- Embroidery floss
- Wool felt for hearts
- Button

REFRIGERATOR LETTER MAGNETS

You can make letters using wool felt and hobby felt. Use pattern 3 on page 124. The letters there have been drawn by freehand. You can look for more letters and different fonts online at www.1001freefonts.com.

Using good textile scissors, start by cutting out the smallest (top) part of the letter. Then cut out the larger sized letter (back). Glue the pieces together with textile glue and place the glued letters under some heavy books to dry. If you use wool felt for one part and hobby felt for the other to make each letter, the finished letters will have the right thickness.

Glue one or two magnets on the back side of each letter. (The strength of the magnet will determine how many you will want use.)

These decorative letters can be used to attach messages, receipts, invitations, notes, or other items onto magnetic boards or refrigerators.

MATERIALS:

- Tracing paper
- Pen
- Hobby felt
- Wool felt
- Textile scissors
- Textile glue
- Magnets, 1 cm in diameter (about ⅜ inch in diameter)

Tip: Children can practice their ABCs and create words with these fun letters!

100%

KEY CHAIN

You can quickly make fun, practical pendants to add to your key chain! It will be so much easier to find your keys, whether they are in your purse or in a drawer, when they are attached to this unique key chain.

To make the owl pendant, start by cutting out two wool felt ovals. Cut out a third oval from another material, such as plastic, leather, or velvet. Sew around the edge of the ovals using a blanket stitch and glue all the pieces together. Cut out the owl and the owl's eyes in wool felt. Glue the eyes on the owl. Draw a beak on the owl with a textile pen. Glue the owl onto the ovals. Attach a metal ring securely to the top of the oval, sewing into it many times. Attach the oval to the key ring.

To make the ball pendant, use wool roving and the wet felting method. First, take a piece of roving and shape it into a ball. Dip the wool ball into soapy water and roll it around in your hand. Repeat the process until your ball is of a desired size. Let it dry. Stitch into the ball from the top to the bottom going around the whole ball to crate a pattern of lines or segments. Attach a sequin and a bead to the bottom of the ball and a ring with a chain to the top. Attach the chain to the key ring.

MATERIALS:

Wool felt
Scissors
A piece of plastic, leather, or velvet
Sewing needle
Embroidery floss/sewing thread
Hobby glue
Tracing paper
Textile pen
Small metal rings
Key ring
Wool roving
Soapy water
Sequin
Bead
Chain

MATERIALS:

Book
Wool felt/hobby felt
Textile scissors
Embroidery floss
Sewing needle
Sewing machine
Textile glue

Create a new, interesting looking cover for an ordinary stiff-backed journal or photo album with a stiff cover. You can use the book as a scrapbook, a journal for yourself, or you can give it to someone as a present.

Cut a sheet of wool felt or hobby felt into a shape and size that will fit your journal cover. The picture shows the felt cut to a size somewhat smaller than the journal's cover.

Decorate the wool felt with words and shapes of your choice. You may want to use some of the patterns available in this book.

Sew all the decorative images onto the wool felt by using a sewing machine or hand stitching.

When you are finshed decorating the wool felt, attach it to the cover of the journal using textile glue.

Place the journal under something heavy until the glue is dry.

MY JOURNAL

MATERIALS:
- Book
- Ruler
- Wool felt/hobby felt
- Textile scissors
- Textile pen
- Wool roving
- Felting needle
- Felting mat
- Sewing needle
- Embroidery floss
- Tracing paper
- Hobby glue

You can completely cover a book with hobby felt or wool felt. Measure the width of both the book's front and back covers, adding the width of the spine. Add 4 inches (10 cm) to each width to create flaps that you can fold under on the inside of the book's cover.

Mark the middle of the felt that will cover the book's front. Draw a heart in this area. Use wool roving and a felting needle to make a textured, soft heart. See pattern 7 on page 126. You can use letters to decorate your cover either by embroidering them free hand, or tracing precise letters onto the cover by using the letter patterns in this book and tracing paper.

Finish decorating the front cover before you glue the felt onto the book. First put some glue on the book's spine, then cover one of the sides with glue and carefully place the felt cover. Work your way from the spine towards the glued cover, smoothing and pressing the felt onto the book. Glue the felt onto the other side of the book using the same process. Finally, glue both flaps to the inside of the covers. Place the book under pressure for a few hours while the glue dries.

You can include a fun, arrow-shaped bookmark to go with your diary. Use pattern 7 on page 126 for your arrow. Sew a blanket stitch around the arrow to finish it off.

Do you have trouble recognizing your own suitcase when it comes sliding by on the baggage belt? A unique and easily noticeable baggage tag could help solve that problem, and help you spot your bag before it circles around again.

Start by cutting out a tag in wool felt using pattern 11 on page 135. Use small, scrap pieces of felt for the window and door decoration on the front of the tag. Place some wool yarn around the door to make a frame. Sew all these pieces in place. Use a bit of roving and a felting needle to felt "home" on the tag. Then cut out the back piece in wool felt. Cut a hole large enough for the name tag to show through, and sew blanket stitches around this opening.

Sew the front and back sides of the tag together using a blanket stitch. Leave an opening at the top in the triangular roof-shaped part so that you can slip in a plastic pocket for the name tag. Use a pen to mark the spot where you want the holes for the ribbon. Punch out a hole in each side of the tag and add grommets, one to the front and one to the back of the tag.

Take an ordinary, clear plastic luggage tag, about 2 x 3 inches (5.5 x 8 cm) and place your name and address information inside the pocket.

Place the plastic pocket inside the felt tag pocket. Use a blanket stitch to sew the "roof" closed.

Thread a ribbon through both holes and attach the tag to your suitcase. Au revoir!

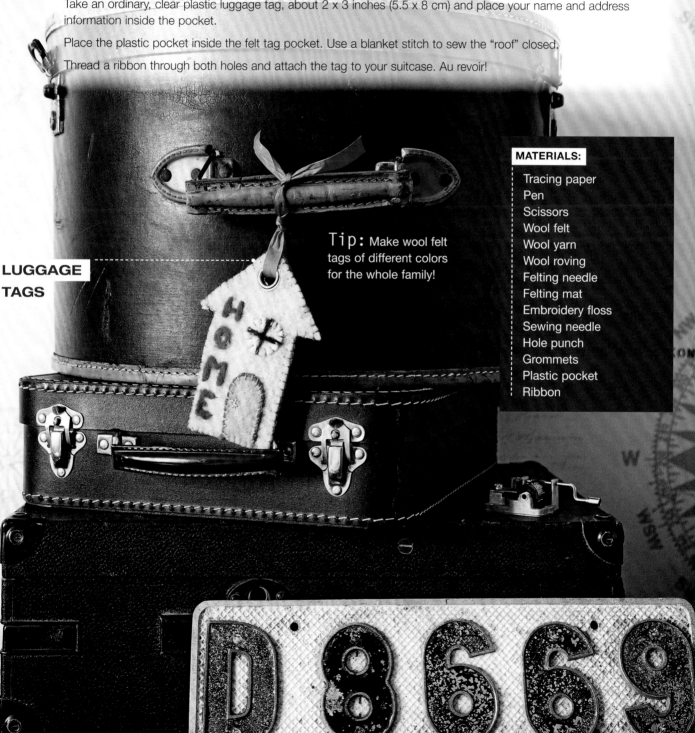

LUGGAGE TAGS

Tip: Make wool felt tags of different colors for the whole family!

MATERIALS:
Tracing paper
Pen
Scissors
Wool felt
Wool yarn
Wool roving
Felting needle
Felting mat
Embroidery floss
Sewing needle
Hole punch
Grommets
Plastic pocket
Ribbon

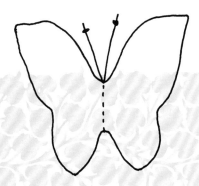

LAPTOP COVER

Wool felt makes great covers for many things because its qualities help protect against damage and dust. Plus, it is nice for a worn laptop to rest in a soft wool felt cover after a hard day of work.

To make a cover, you must first measure the width and length of your laptop/tablet. Make the top piece 2⅜ inches (6 cm) longer than the other piece of felt. This extra length is for a flap. Make sure to add seam allowances to your measurements where the pieces of felt will be sewn together. Cut out two pieces of wool felt that fit these measurements. You may want to use two different colors of felt. The felt cover shown in the picture measures 11 x 8 inches (28 x 20 cm) (10 ¼ inches (26 cm) on the front) plus seam allowances.

Cut out 13 wool felt circles with a 1½ inch (4 cm) diameter (see pattern on page 123), and cut out one wool felt butterfly using the pattern on this page.

Sew a blanket stitch with embroidery floss around each circle. Pin 11 circles in place on the front of the wool felt cover, and attach them to the cover with basting stitches. Use blanket stitches to sew around the butterfly. Finish it off by leaving two threads with knots at the end for the antennas. Use a sewing machine to sew the front and back sides of your wool felt cover together, right sides facing. Turn the cover right side out, and sew blanket stitches around the opening. Attach the two last circles to the back of the cover. Attach one circle to the main body of the cover, and attach the other felt circle, with a decorative button in the center, to the flap.

Sew on two large snap buttons for closure.

MATERIALS:

Ruler
Wool felt in 2 colors
Textile scissors
Tracing paper
Pen
Embroidery floss
Sewing needle
Sewing machine
Decorative button
2 large snap buttons

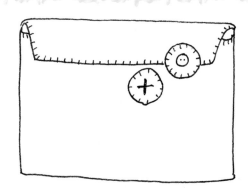

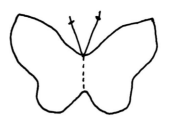

You can easily make a soft, durable case in wool felt for your camera. Start by measuring the length, width, and thickness of your camera. Using these measurements, and cut out one piece of wool felt that will be both the front and back sides of the camera case. Fold the wool felt in half and mark the center. Cut out nine small, round wool felt pieces for the back of the cover. As shown in the photo, sew a grid pattern over the circles to attach them to the part of the felt that will be the back of the case. Cut out two circles in felt, one with a 1⅛ inch (3 cm) diameter, and the smaller circle has a ⅝ inch (1.5 cm) diameter. Pin the smaller circle on top of the larger one, and sew them in place with a needle and thread on the part of the felt that will be the front of the case. Fold the wool felt piece in half, right sides facing, and sew the side and bottom together. Turn the case right side out, and attach a wool felt tab to the back of it. The tab should be ¾ x 1⅝ inches (2 x 4 cm). Attach a snap button to the tab and to the front of the case. Cut out a wool felt butterfly using the pattern on this page. Sew small blanket stitches around the butterfly, and finish it off with thread antennas as described in the previous pattern, page 42. Attach the butterfly to the tab at the front of the camera case.

CAMERA CASE

MATERIALS:

Ruler
Wool felt in 2 colors
Textile scissors
Embroidery floss
Sewing needle
Sewing machine
Button
Fiberfill
Cell phone strap

MATERIALS:

Ruler
Wool felt in 2 colors
Textile scissors
Sewing machine
Embroidery floss
Sewing needle
Snap button

CELL PHONE CASE

To make the wool felt case for your cell phone, you must first measure the cell phone's length and width. Use these measurements to cut out two pieces of felt, one pink and one gray. Cut out 12 small, round felt pieces, and decorate the pink piece of wool felt with these circles. Baste them in place so that they will not move while you are sewing. Using a sewing machine to sew a grid pattern over the circles to attach them to the wool felt piece. Remove the basting stitches as needed. Attach a wool felt tab measuring ¾ x 1⅝ inches (2 x 4 cm) to the pink wool felt piece. Make a small button hole in the tab.

Make a small, wool felt heart that you can use as a decoration for your cell phone strap or to decorate the wool felt case. Cut out two wool felt hearts using the pattern on this page. Next cut out a small circle in wool felt. Place a little fiberfill between the two hearts, and stitch them together with blanket stitches. Sew the small, wool felt circle onto the middle of the heart. Attach the heart to the ring on the cell phone strap.

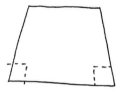

CHAIR COVER

Fashion trends come and go, and if you have a nice chair that you want to keep for a long time, you can make it current with a removable cover. A cover made from wool felt will make the chair feel warm and comfortable. And for some fun, visual interest, you can add a felted letter.

Make a pattern before you cut out the wool felt for your cover. Cut about 4-4¾ inches (10-12 cm) beyond the edge of the seat on all sides, except the side towards the back of the chair (the new cover should be flush with the back of the chair). Place the wool felt over the seat and mark the location of each leg using pins. Fold the felt under at each corner in the front, pin, and sew. Remove the cover and turn it to the right side. Transfer initials and /or numbers onto the cover using tracing paper. Place a small amount of roving over the traced letter or number, and felt it onto the cover using a felting needle. Place a Styrofoam sheet under the wool felt while you are working the needle to protect the surface below. When you have finished felting the letter or number, place a moist cloth over the image and press with an iron to enhance the motif. Attach two ribbons, each 12 inches (30 cm) long, on each side of the cover in the back, a total of four ribbons per cover.

Tip: You can find different styles of letters at www.1001freefonts.com. Print them in the sizes you want to create your own patterns. See also pattern 9 on page 123 for the M shown here.

BARSTOOL COVER

If the cover on your barstool is worn and ugly, you can easily make a new one using wool felt.

Remove the stool's back support with a screw driver. Use an old sheet, or something similar, to make a pattern for the new seat cover. Place the sheet on the bar stool seat and trace on it the pattern pieces you will need by following the shape of the seat. Cut out all the drawn pattern pieces, lay them on wool felt, and cut out all the pieces with a small seam allowance. You do not need much of a seam allowance, because the wool felt will stretch when used. Sew together the two felt pieces for the bar stool seat on a sewing machine. Turn the new cover over with the right side facing out. Pull the new cover over the barstool seat and fasten it to the underside of the seat with a staple gun and staples.

To ensure that your new seat cover looks even, attach the cover using one staple at each side in a straight line across from each other. Then staple on each side of the first two staples. Continue to attach the cover by stapling around the whole seat, making sure that the new cover is taut. The thickness of the wool felt will determine the longevity of your new cover. If you use thick wool felt to cover your stool, it will last longer than a cover made with thin wool felt.

MATERIALS:

Wool felt/felted wool garment
Screw driver
Old sheet
Marker
Textile scissors
Sewing machine
Staple gun

Upcycle Tip: Machine wash a thick wool sweater on hot and it will become dense and compact. Pull the felted sweater over a barstool seat and attach it to the seat with staples.

SQUARE FLOOR
PILLOW

A pillow is easy to hide and take out when you need some extra seating. It can work as a movable seat and as a side table for the living room or a child's room. You can make the structure for this pillow out of newspapers. This is a good way to recycle old issues.

Build your pillow by tightly stacking newspapers to your desired height and securing the stack with packaging tape around all sides.

Add a 1-2 inches (3-5 cm) thick foam cushion on top of the newspapers for sitting comfort.

Measure width and height of each side of the newspaper cube, and use the measurements to cut out all the pieces in wool felt. You will need five pieces. Make sure to add a seam allowance for all seams. It does not have to be big, because the wool stretches quite a bit.

For our cube we used:

2 yellow sides 13⅜ x 16⅛ inches (34 x 41 cm)
2 gray sides 13⅜ x 11 inches (34 x 28 cm)
1 black side 11 x 16⅛ inches (28 x 41 cm)

To make an "&" sign for decoration, see pattern 12 on page 132.

Place the cut out "&" pattern on the wool felt and trace around it with a textile marker. Position a felt mat under the felt where the sign will be located, and felt the "&" symbol using wool roving. You may want to use a black roving for the edges and a gray roving to fill in the symbol. Sew all the felt pieces together on the right side. The seams should be on the outside of the cube.

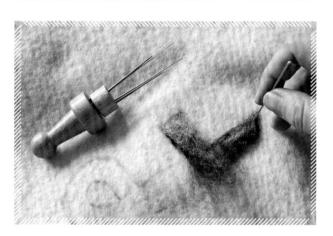

MATERIALS:

Newspapers
Packing tape
Measuring tape
Foam for seat
3 colors of wool felt
Sewing machine
Parchment paper/pen
Wool roving
Felting needle
Felting mat

MATERIALS:

Wool felt
Textile scissors
Sewing needle
Thread
Sequins
Metal wire
Beads

FLOWERPOT COVER

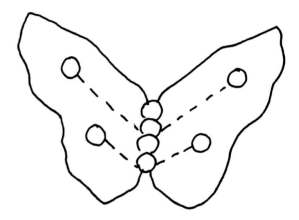

You can easily change the look of your flowerpots by covering them with unique, felted flowerpot covers. They are very easy to make and are a colorful addition to any table or shelf. Try choosing decorations to reflect the seasons or other themes.

Measure the height and the circumference of the pot or the container you want to cover. Then add to the height of the cover the length of the points of the crown. The points of the crown are measured from the rim of the pot. Allow for a ⅜ inch (1 cm) overlap in the width of the cover, attach the sides together, and sew with small stitches, or add ¾ inch (2 cm) so that you can use Velcro to fasten the sides together.

Decorate the cover using beads and sequins. A wool felt butterfly in a contrasting color would look great as a decoration for the pot cover, or you could attach it directly to the plant itself. Use a thin metal wire and wrap it around the plant stem to attach the butterfly to the plant.

You can also make a cover for a glass tea light holder. Be very careful and do not make the points of the crown too tall, because they could become a fire hazard.

Make the butterfly by cutting it out of wool felt. Decorate it with embroidery stitches and add sequins.

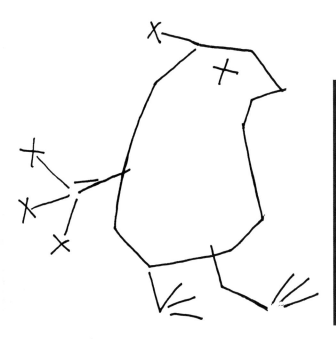

WHIMSICAL PILLOWS

A house shaped pillow is a fun addition to any collection of differently shaped pillows that have been made from old skirts and sweaters!

Choose wool felt in different colors for your project. I have used a combination of felted wool garment and wool felt for the depicted pillows. To make your own pillows, start out by drawing and cutting out templates using paper. Place the different house shapes on your felted fabrics and cut them out. Sew all the shapes for the front piece of you pillow together. Decorate the front of the pillow with small felt pieces, embroidery, and needle felted decorations. Sew the pillow's sides together using a blanket stitch. Make sure that the wrong sides of the pillow are facing each other. Leave an opening at the bottom of the pillow and fill it with fiberfill. Adjust the amount of fiberfill to get the firmness you want. The more you stuff your pillow, the firmer it will feel. Pin the opening and stitch it shut with blanket stitches.

Tip: If you have unused pillow inserts, you can cut them open and use the contents to fill pillows that are not rectangular or square.

Narrow Pillow:
13 inches (33 cm) from the bottom of the house to the roof's eaves; 12¼ inches (31 cm) from the roof's eaves to the chimney; 9 inches (23 cm) pillow's width; 2 inches (5 cm) chimney's width.

Wide Pillow:
12¼ inches (31 cm) from the bottom of the house to the roof's eaves; 9½ inches (24 cm) from the roof's eaves to the chimney; 12⅝ inches (32 cm) pillow's width; 15 inches (38 cm) the width of the roof at the eaves.

MATERIALS:

Solid colored pillow
Wool felt
Hobby felt
Textile scissors
Embroidery floss
Sewing needle
Pins

This flower-covered pillow is a good project to tackle when you are feeling a little bit more ambitious. It may take a little longer to complete this project, but the results will be very impressive!

Use a solid colored pillow that you already own, and give it a brand new look!

Start by cutting out flowers in different sizes from colored wool felt or hobby felt. Sew around the flowers' edges using a blanket stitch before you attach them to the pillow. Experiment with different kinds of embroidery stitches to decorate the flowers. You may, for example, want to sew basting stitches around some flowers. Cut out some felt circles with fringes and small felt leaves. You can stack the wool felt flowers and other shapes on top of each other.

Place all the finished flowers and leaves on the pillow, and pin them down. Make adjustments to your layout, so that your flowers are positioned in a harmonious and balanced way. Sew all the flowers and leaves to the pillow using small stitches.

PATCHWORK PILLOW

MATERIALS:

Wool felt/felted wool garment
Measuring tape
Textile scissors
Pins
Sewing machine
Cotton thread
Sewing needle
Pillow insert
Snaps
Yarn

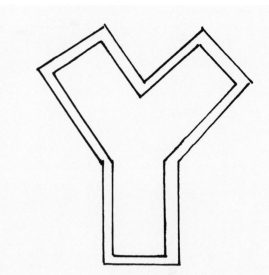

Take an old wool sweater, wash it in the washing machine on hot, and you will create a fun, repurposed material, useful for many projects. Simply cut out squares from the felted garment, place the squares in a row, and sew them together to make a patchwork pillow. Just like that, you have created something entirely new from an old sweater!

First, you must decide how big you want your pillow.

Take the total length you have decided on for the pillow and divide this length by 3. This measurement will be the length of each patch. Use the same procedure for the height of the pillow. Make sure to include a small seam allowance for each patch. The pillow in the picture measures about 20 x 24 inches (50 x 60 cm).

Cut out all the patches you will need and arrange them to create a pleasing pattern. Pin them together and sew, one row at a time. Keep the seam allowances on the right side of the pillow. The back of the pillow can be made from one single piece of fabric.

Cut out felt letters and attach them to the front of the pillow using small stitches. Refer to page 36 for how to make the letters.

Place the pillow's front and back sides on top of each other with the back sides of the fabrics towards each other. Stitch around the edges using a ⅜ inch (1 cm) seam allowance. Make sure to leave an opening for the pillow insert. You can attach snaps at the opening to close it.

If you do not want to use snaps for the closure, you can hand stitch the opening shut after you have placed the pillow insert.

For a fun look, add tassels to you finished pillow! Cut out 6 lengths of felt measuring ⅜ x 6 inches (1 x 15 cm) to make the tassels. Fold the strips in half, wrap a piece of yarn several times around the folded end of the strips, and sew to fasten. Then sew the tassels onto the corners of the pillow.

MATERIALS:
Parchment paper
Pen
Scissors
Wool felt
String of lights

FLOWER GARLAND WITH LIGHTS

Most people think of using a string of lights only at Christmas time. However, there are many other evenings during the year when a few strings of light would add beautiful ambiance. By adding wool felt flowers to an ordinary string of lights, you will get a unique, decorative garland that will brighten your life at anytime of the year! Use pattern 20 on page 122.

Cut out flowers in two different sizes from two or three differently colored pieces of felt. You will need to cut a small cross at the center of each flower to slip them onto the string of lights. First thread the larger flower onto the light and then add the smaller flower. Make sure that you do not place the flowers close to the light bulbs.

Note! Do not leave the string of lights on when you are not at home.

COLORFUL
LAMP SHADE

Wool felt can be used as a lamp shade cover for a brand new look. If you have an old lamp shade lying around, you can easily remove the old cover and use the frame to make a new lampshade with colorful wool felt. First make a pattern using wool felt. You may want to use four to six equally sized pieces of felt in different colors. Measure the shade's height and make sure that the felt pieces are long enough to wrap around the top and bottom of the frame. Place the pieces of wool felt next to each other in a sequence that you like, and pin them together with the seam allowances towards you. To make sure that the new lamp shade cover is taut over the lamp shade frame, pull the wool felt tightly over the frame as you pin the pieces together. Sew the side seams together with double embroidery floss. Attach the new cover to the top and the bottom of the frame with basting stitches. Finish off by adding flower decorations.

One Felted Sweater = Four Projects

Take one wool sweater, felt in the washing machine in very hot water, and you can transform it into many new, wonderful things.

FINGERLESS GLOVES

Cut out from the felted wool sweater a piece measuring about 9 inches (23 cm) wide for the wrist, and 6⅝ inches (17 cm) long. You may want to check these measurements before you cut to make sure that the fingerless gloves will fit. Cut out a second piece of the same size from the felted sweater. Make sure that you cut both pieces from the same pattern area on the sweater so the fingerless gloves will match and be symmetrical. Sew the sides together on each glove. Finish off the fingerless gloves' edges by crocheting borders to embellish them. Pick up stitches around the edge of the fingerless glove at the wrist by using a # 2.5 (US B or 1) crochet needle. (Sometimes it can be difficult to pick up stitches from a felted garment, but do not give up!) Start by crocheting two or three rows of single crochet stitches, and then finish off with a row of picots. You can make the picots by crocheting three chain stitches, then crocheting one single stitch back into the first chain stitch. At the opposite end of the fingerless glove, you can finish off the edge by crocheting a simple row of single crochet stitches. Your fingerless gloves are now ready to keep you warm on those extra chilly days.

BAG

This unique bag measures 10 inches (25 cm) high in the middle and 11 inches (28 cm) on the sides. It is 12½ inches (32 cm) wide where the handles attach and increases to 15 inches (38 cm) wide at the bottom of the bag.

Using the measurements above, cut out the two pieces of felted wool for the bag from the front and the back of the sweater. Include seam allowances on the sides and bottom and an extra 5 inches (13 cm) at the top. Sew the sides and bottom of the bag together with the right sides of the felted fabric facing each other. Leave a 6 inches (15 cm) opening near the top at each side. Turn the bag inside out. Fold the seam allowances at the side openings towards the inside of the bag and stitch in place using a basting stitch. When you have finished sewing around the openings at the sides of the bag, make a pocket at the top of the bag on both sides by folding down the felted wool 2½ inches (6 cm). Stitch the fold in place. Slip a strong, flexible branch into the pocket. Bend the branch into a handle shape and where the branch overlaps, tightly wrap the joint with a metal wire. Pull the joint into the pocket so that it will not be visible. Repeat the same process for the second handle. To embellish your bag and to create an interesting color contrast, sew a seam using basting stitches along the bottom of the bag. Use a bright, neon colored yarn for this seam. Decorate the bag some more by adding a row of yarn bobbles across the middle of the purse using the same neon colored yarn. First make one yarn knot, then add another knot on top of the first one, then add one more, and you will have made a yarn bobble. Repeat.

As a last touch, wrap some of the yarn around the handle and tie it in a bow. Your fun, decorative bag is now finished.

63

HEART

To make a heart from your felted sweater, use pattern 22 on page 123 and cut out one piece for the front and one for the back of the heart. Sew around each of the heart pieces using a blanket stitch. Then sew the pieces together with a basting stitch, leave an opening, and stuff the heart with fiberfill. Close the opening using basting stitches.

When you have finished making your heart, cut out four wool felt circles in different colors. See pattern on the next page.

Cut snips into each circle around the circumference to create a fringe. Fold the circle in two at the center, and then fold it in two again so that you get a quarter of a circle.

Secure the shape with a needle and thread. When you have completed making all the circles into quarter circles, assemble them into a ball and sew them together.

Next, make a wet felted ball (see page 7).

Let the ball dry.

Use a strong cotton thread and a darning needle to thread the felted ball onto the thread. Add a piece of yellow felt and the fringe ball, and fasten the cotton thread to the point at the bottom of the heart. Attach a new thread at the top of the heart. You are now ready to hang your felted heart on an armoire or in a window.

HEADBAND

The felted sweater's wide collar can be repurposed as a fancy headband. You may want to fold under the collar's edge and stitch it in place with basting stitches to create a finished look, or you can just leave a raw edge.

Make a decoration using wool felt flowers to embellish your headband. Cut out in wool felt the star-shaped patterns below. Cut snips into the shapes around the edges to create a fringed look. Choose a couple of differently colored felts and cut out three circles using the circle pattern above. Snip into the circles' edges as well, and fold each one in half, and then into quarters. Make a flower by sewing the three circle quarters together. Attach the felt flower to the star-shapes by stitching them all together, and add a brooch pin to the back of the decoration. Pin the decoration to your headband.

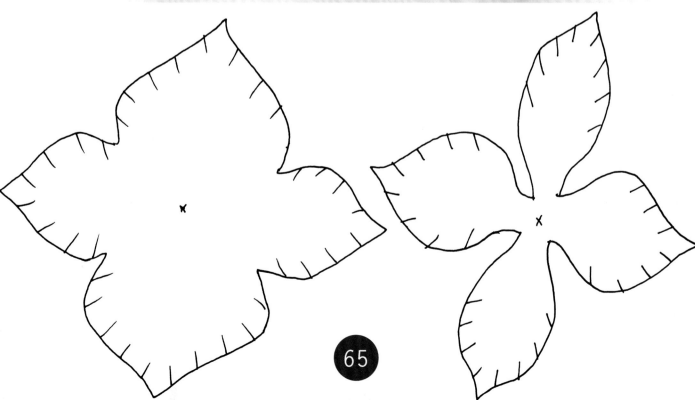

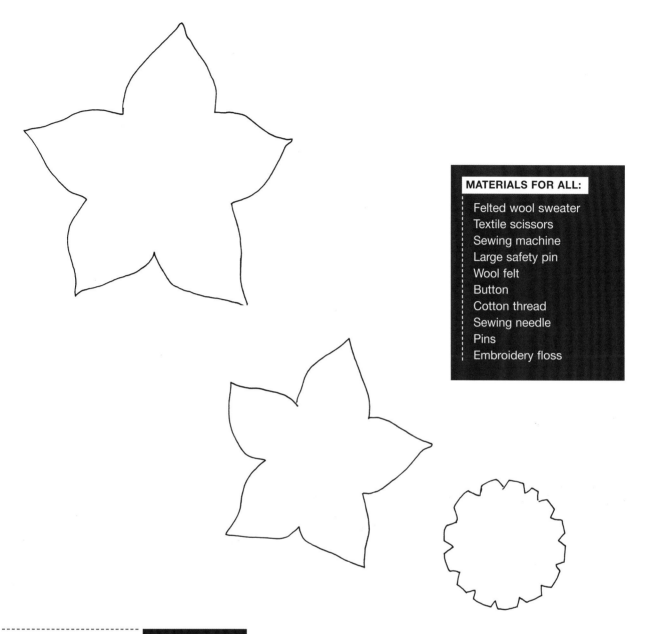

DOG COAT

A thick coat made from a felted wool sweater will keep your dog warm as the temperature falls. As this picture shows, we used a wool sweater with a nice collar to make a coat for our dog, Freya. To make the coat, cut out felted sweater's back side and the area around the neck. This piece is large enough to cover a dog's back and stomach, and to provide an overlap at the front around the neck.

Sew an about 5 inches (13 cm) long seam under the coat in the stomach area to help the coat stay in place. Use scissors and cut a nice rounded edge from the seam up towards the back of the coat. You can use a safety pin to fasten the coat together at the front. A nice flower decoration made from wool felt will make the coat extra special.

Make the simple flower decoration by using the patterns on this page and wool felt in several shades of gray. When you have cut out all the pieces, lay all the shapes on top of each other and sew them together. Attach a button in the center of the felt flower. Sew a brooch pin to the back of the flower, and pin it on the coat.

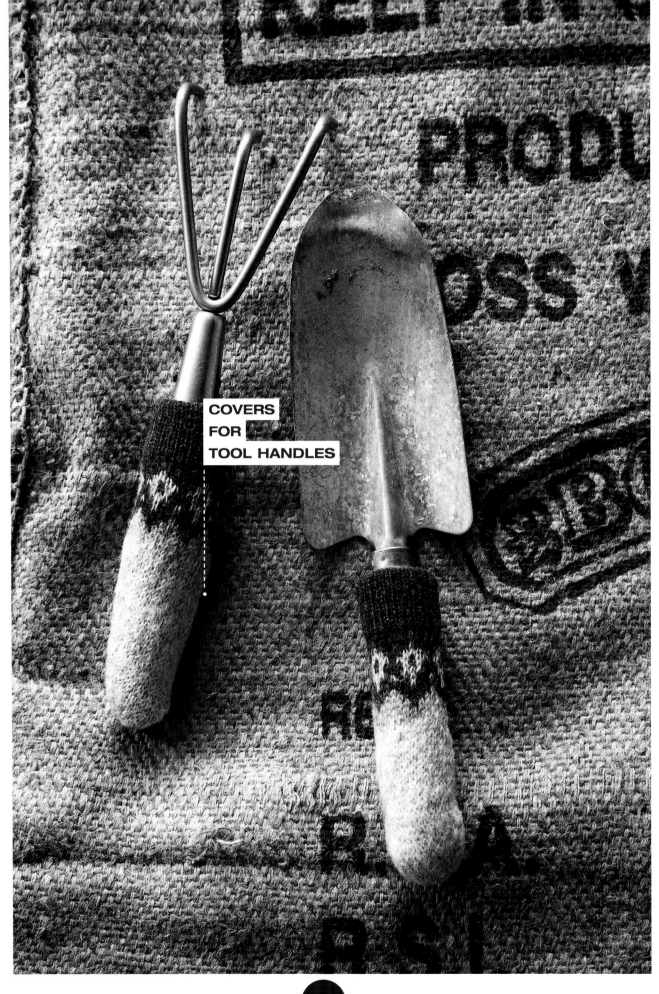

COVERS
FOR
TOOL HANDLES

68

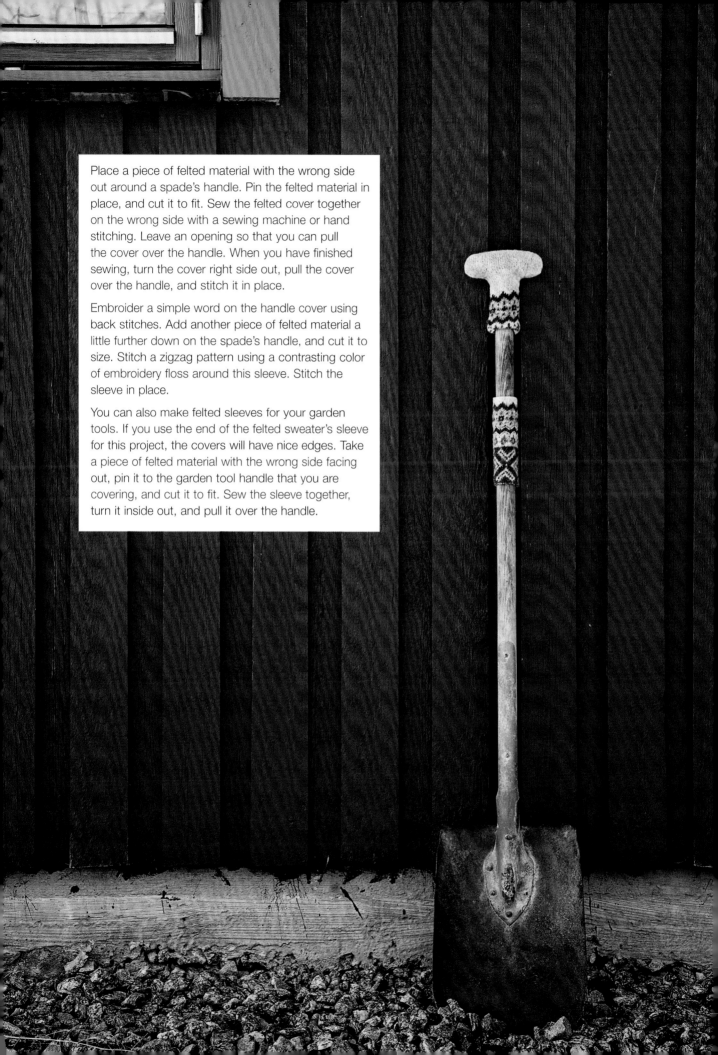

Place a piece of felted material with the wrong side out around a spade's handle. Pin the felted material in place, and cut it to fit. Sew the felted cover together on the wrong side with a sewing machine or hand stitching. Leave an opening so that you can pull the cover over the handle. When you have finished sewing, turn the cover right side out, pull the cover over the handle, and stitch it in place.

Embroider a simple word on the handle cover using back stitches. Add another piece of felted material a little further down on the spade's handle, and cut it to size. Stitch a zigzag pattern using a contrasting color of embroidery floss around this sleeve. Stitch the sleeve in place.

You can also make felted sleeves for your garden tools. If you use the end of the felted sweater's sleeve for this project, the covers will have nice edges. Take a piece of felted material with the wrong side facing out, pin it to the garden tool handle that you are covering, and cut it to fit. Sew the sleeve together, turn it inside out, and pull it over the handle.

MATERIALS:

Tracing paper
Pen
Wool felt/felted wool garment
Textile scissors
Sewing machine
Wool roving
Soapy water
Wool yarn
Sewing needle
Thread
Ribbon 17¾ inches (45 cm)

Trace patterns 25A (two pieces) and pattern 25B on pages 130 and 131 onto tracing paper and cut them out. (You will need a total of six pattern pieces for one pair of mittens.) Place the patterns on wool felt or, as we have done, on a felted wool garment. If you are placing the pattern pieces on a felted sweater with different patterns, colors, and textures, you must be careful to place both the right and the left (mirrored) pattern pieces in the same area so that the two mittens will match. Cut out the pattern pieces for the mittens. Make sure that you include a seam allowance for each pattern piece. Start by sewing the two pattern pieces 25A together. They make up the palm side of the mitten. With the right sides facing each other, pin the marked point 1 on one piece to the marked point 1 on the other piece. Then pin the marked point 2 on one piece to the marked point 2 on the other piece, and do the same for the marked points 3. Place some more pins in the area between 1, 2, and 3, and then sew a seam between 1 and 2. Next place the palm side of the mitten (the sewn patterns pieces 25A) on top of the top side of the mitten (pattern piece 25B), right sides facing, and pin together at x on both pieces. Match marked point 4 to the corresponding point 4, pin around the mitten, and sew.

Repeat the whole process to make the other mitten. Use the same pattern pieces and place them mirrored on the felt. These mittens are approximately a size 8. If you want smaller or larger mittens, resize the patterns accordingly.

Make four small, felted wool balls using the wet felting method, see page 7. Let the felted balls dry. Cut a piece of wool yarn about 7 inches (18 cm) long for each mitten, and sew one felted ball to each end. Attach the yarn with the felted balls at the top of the mitten. Sew a ribbon, about 8⅝ inches (22 cm) long, on the top side of the mitten. Use a tight basting stitch or overcasting stitch on both edges of the ribbon to attach it.

MITTENS WITH RIBBON

Create beautifully decorated mittens with colorful yarns and a felting needle. No sewing is necessary. Choose solid colored mittens, and use different qualities of yarn, such as wool and mohair, for this project. You do not have to use wool roving.

Trace the pattern on this page onto tracing paper and transfer it onto your mitten. Slip a felting mat in side the mitten, and start felting the wool yarn onto the mitten following the pattern. It is best to start at the bottom of the pattern, and then work your way from the right to the left and up. Repeat the same process for the other mitten. If you are not satisfied with the results, or think that the pattern does not quite match on the two mittens, you can easily redo the parts that are not working. Just pull the yarn loose and re-felt the area. If you are concerned that it may be too difficult to do this kind of felting, you may be surprised by how easy it is with a little practice.

DECORATED MITTENS

MATERIALS:

Tracing paper
Pen
Wool mittens
Wool yarn
Mohair yarn
Felting needle
Felting mat

GLOVE CUFFS WITH DRAGONFLY

Measure around your wrist, and cut out a piece of wool felt using the measurement of your wrist's circumference as the width and 4¾ inches (12 cm) as the height. Make the cuffs glove wide enough, so that you can pull them over your hands. Shape the edges at the wrist by cutting a zigzag border that is about ⅝ inch (1.5 cm) deep. Trace the dragonfly pattern on this page onto tracing paper. Place the tracing paper with the pattern on top of the wool felt, and trace the image. Transfer the image to the felt. Felt the dragonfly image onto the felt piece with turquoise wool roving. Decorate the dragonfly with small pieces of white and green wool roving. Embroider additional details on the dragonfly with lilac embroidery floss. Finish off the zigzag border at the wrist by sewing blanket stitches around the edges. Attach one sequin at each point on the zigzag border. Pin each cuff's sides together, and sew using a basting stitch. If you prefer a tighter fit, attach Velcro to the two sides, on the front and the back, and use the Velcro to close the glove cuffs around your wrist.

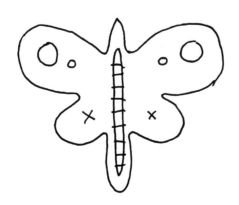

MATERIALS:

Wool felt
Textile scissors
Wool roving
Felting needle
Felting mat
Decorative elastic band
Sewing thread
Pins
Sewing machine

GLOVE CUFFS WITH DOTS

Find two pieces of wool felt that are about 6½ inches (16 cm) long and wrap one piece around your wrist. Place markers on the felt that is around your wrist when you have decided how tightly you want your glove cuffs to fit. You now have the cuff's width. Add a seam allowance on both sides of each cuff's width. It is best to have a snug fit and a rather long length.

Make sure that you are able to pull these glove cuffs over your hand, because the ends will be sewn together. Sew the wool felt pieces together after you have finished felting on the decorations so that you can keep the felt flat on the felting mat. Make small balls from small pieces of wool roving, and felt them onto the wool felt with a felting needle. Work the needle several times through the wool roving ball to make sure that it is securely attached to the wool felt. You can choose how many dots you want to create. When you are satisfied with the result, pin a decorative elastic band to each cuff's edge. Use a sewing machine set on a large zigzag stitch setting and a sewing thread in a contrasting color to attach the elastic band to the wool felt. Fold the felt in half with the right sides facing each other, and sew a straight seam along the length of the felt. Turn the glove cuffs right side out. You are now good to go.

MATERIALS:

Wool felt
Lace/lace cuff
Sewing thread
Sewing needle
Fabric button
Thin ribbon
Beads

GLOVE CUFFS WITH LACE

To make these glove cuffs, start with two pieces of white wool felt 4 x 6½ inches (10 x 16 cm), and decorate them with lace. Cut out two pieces of lace as wide as your pieces of wool felt. Attach a fabric button on one side of each lace piece, and make a loop with a thin ribbon on the other side of the lace. Sew the lace pieces in place on the wool felt. You can decorate the lace by sewing on some pretty beads. If you prefer, it would be just as easy to make lace glove cuffs by removing two lace cuffs from an old blouse and attaching them directly onto the wool felt pieces.

Use two pieces of wool felt measuring about 4 x 7½ inches (10 x 19 cm) wide for these elegant glove cuffs. Check the width by measuring around your wrists. The felt pieces should be large enough so that the edges can overlap, and be fastened together with Velcro.

Cut out two thin lengths of felt for each cuff from the same wool felt you used before. The strips should measure about ⅜ x 7½ inches (1 x 19 cm). Attach one strip to the top and one to the bottom of the cuff with a zigzag stitch setting on your sewing machine.

To decorate your glove cuffs, chose three different ribbons by mixing ribbons with an ethnic pattern and silk ribbons. Make sure that the ribbons go well together and that they are about 7½ inches (19 cm) long. You may want to choose a red/white color scheme as shown in the picture.

The ribbon that you have chosen for the middle of the cuff should be 1¾ inches (4.5 cm) longer then the others so that you can make a tab, which will be used to close the cuff. Leave the extra ribbon length on one side of the glove cuff, fold it in half, and stitch the end in place. Fasten one side of a piece of Velcro to the under-side of the ribbon tab, and attach another the other side on the other end of the glove cuff at a matching location. You can attach all the ribbons to the wool felt by using either a sewing machine or by hand stitching. Add antique mother-of-pearl buttons and appliques to the middle ribbon to finish off the look.

ELEGANT GLOVE CUFFS

MATERIALS:

Wool felt
Textile scissors
Sewing machine
Woven ribbons/ribbons
  with ethnic patterns
Silk ribbons/silk textiles,
  or similar
Sewing needle
Velcro
Buttons
Appliques
Thread

Start with a piece of black wool felt measuring 3⅜ x 7½ inches (8.5 x 19 cm) to make these fun glove cuffs. Wrap the piece of felt around your wrist to make sure that the piece is wide enough. You should be able to overlap the edges and have enough felt at the overlap to fasten Velcro pieces for closure. Choose five ribbons in happy colors that are 8 inches (20 cm) long, and pin them to the wool felt. Fold the ribbons under in line with the felt's edge at one end of the piece. Sew the ribbon ends in place on this side. Fold the ribbon ends under, and attach them to the felt ⅜ inch (1 cm) from the edge at the opposite side. Finish attaching the ribbons to the felt by using a sewing machine and metallic thread for additional embellishment. Attach Velcro pieces at the edges of the cuff, on both sides, to close it around your wrist. Sew festive buttons on the ribbons for extra sparkle and interest. Repeat the process for a matching glove cuff, and you have a pair.

GLOVE CUFFS WITH RIBBONS

MATERIALS:

Wool felt
5 Ribbons, about 8 inches (20 cm) each
Sewing needle
Metallic sewing thread
Sewing machine
Velcro
Buttons

MATERIALS:

Wool hat
Tracing paper
Pen
Wool felt/hobby felt
Textile scissors
Textile glue
Sewing needle
Thread
Embroidery floss
Beads

WINTER HAT WITH FLOWERS

The hat in the picture started out without any shape, and it was too large. We felted it in the washing machine on hot, and it became denser, smaller, and more usable. To finish off our new creation, we decorated the hat with a few wool felt flowers, and it became as good as brand new.

Trace the pattern for the roses on this page and cut them out in a spiral shape (see page 90).

To make your roses, start by rolling each flower from the center of the spiral and work your way out. The rose will have a somewhat built-up shape. Add a little glue to the bottom of the flowers, and sew them onto the hat adding a bead at the center of each rose.

Attach felt leaves to the hat using basting stitches. If you want to, you can also decorate the hat by sewing cross stitches around it.

FUN HATS
FOR KIDS

These fun, felt hats with faces on the top are just right for colder days.

Use pattern 26 on page 127. You can copy the pattern with the drawings and text onto tracing paper. The depicted pattern is sized for children 2–4 years old. Add ⅝ inch (1.5 cm) around the whole pattern to make a larger hat that will work well for children that are 5+ years old. Cut out two pieces in wool felt. Sew the pieces together with a blanket stitch, and continue the same stitch around the edge of the opening. Gather two pieces of tulle 4 x 2½ inches (10 x 6 cm) each, and attach one piece of tulle to each "ear" as you sew the hat pieces together.

Glue on eyes and a felt beak. Place a piece of wool roving inside the top of the hat to fill out the shape, and secure it in place.

MATERIALS:

Tracing paper
Pen
Wool felt
Embroidery floss
Sewing needle
Tulle
Hobby glue
Plastic eyes
Wool roving or fiberfill

Use the patterns 32 (cut 2 pieces) and 32A on pages 138 and 139 to make these fun, warm slippers. Start by tracing the patterns onto parchment paper. If you want different sizes than those given, you can reduce or enlarge the patterns. Place the patterns on wool felt and cut out the felt pieces for one slipper. Repeat for second slipper. Remember to make the second slipper a mirrored image of the first slipper, so that you end up with a left and right slipper. Add a very small seam allowance to each pattern, because you do not need much. Choose extra-thick wool felt for the soles, for example, an about ³/₁₆ inch (5 mm) thick felt or use double-heavy felt.

Pin the felt piece for the heel to the sole of the slipper. Adjust the seams so that the slipper fits your foot. It is best to make a snug fit, because the wool relaxes as it is worn, and your slipper can become too big. Pin the top felt piece to the sole piece. Follow the numbers on the pattern, lining up the marked point 1 on one piece with the marked point 1 on the other piece. Repeat the same process with the marked points 2. Sew the pieces together with double embroidery floss using a blanket stitch. The wool felt's density will determine your slipper's fit. A denser felt will give a better fit. If you choose to use regular wool felt, pull the wool felt as you stitch a little together. When you have finished sewing your slippers, decorate them with wool felt hearts, lace, buttons, crochet flowers, textile decorations, tulle or whatever else you can think of.

Use puffy paint on the soles of your slippers so they have better grip. Turn the slippers up side down, and make any patterns you want with the puffy paint. Let the slippers dry for 6 hours or according to the manufacturer's instructions. Iron lightly after the puffy paint is completely dry. Your slippers are now ready to wear.

T i p s : Make many slippers of different styles and sizes, and keep them in a basket by the front door so guests can use them!

To make another version of the slippers, you can sew bias tape around the slippers' heals and openings.

MATERIALS:

Parchment paper
Pen
Wool felt/Nepal wool felt
Heavy, thick felt
Textile scissors
Pins
Bias tape
Sewing needle
Double embroidery floss
Crochet flower decorations
Puffy Paint

FELT SLIPPERS FOR KIDS

MATERIALS:

Parchment paper
Pen
Wool felt/Nepal wool felt
Heavy, thick felt
Textile scissors
Pins
Bias tape
Sewing needle
Double embroidery floss
Tulle
Decorative elements
Puffy Paint

Use the same instructions as on page 84 and pattern 33 on pages 136 and 137 to make slippers for children. If you want to edge the slippers' openings with bias tape, sew it onto the wool felt pieces before you attach them to the soles. Use a blanket stitch for sewing the pieces together, and decorate the slippers with crocheted mini-flowers, decorative buttons (see photo on opposite page), tulle (see above), or other decorations you may have.

Adding Tulle

If you are going to use tulle as a decoration for a slipper, cut out two strips in different colors. One strip should be 2 x 17¾ inches (5 x 45 cm) long, and the other strip should be 1½ x 13¾ inches (4 x 35 cm) long. Place the strips on top of each other, aligning them at one long edge, and sew a seam with large basting stitches along this edge. Make sure to fasten your thread before you start sewing. When you have finished sewing, pull on the thread to cinch up the tulle and make a ruffle. Fasten the pulled thread, twist the ruffle into a circle, and secure the shape with a few stitches. Attach textile flowers in coordinating colors to the middle of the ruffle before you sew it onto the slipper.

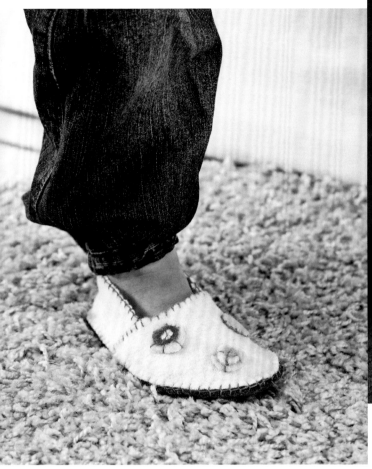

Use pattern 34 on page 133 for these adorable baby slippers. Start by tracing the pattern onto parchment paper, and cutting out the pattern pieces. Remember to make the second slipper a mirrored image of the first slipper, so that you end up with a left and right slippers. Place the pattern pieces on wool felt, and cut out all the pieces. Pin the pieces together lining up marked point 1 on one piece with marked point 1 on the other piece. Repeat the same process for the marked points 2 and 3. Sew around the entire slipper using a blanket stitch. To decorate the slippers, cut out two small hearts in felt for each slipper. Run a cotton thread through the center of each heart and the slipper, and tie it in place with a knot. Use puffy paint and make a grippy pattern on the bottom of the soles.

Tip: You can write a child's name on the bottom of the soles with the puffy paint. This special detail will make the slippers a wonderful gift for a newborn baby!

FELT SLIPPERS FOR BABIES

(see photo on page 85)

MATERIALS:

Parchment paper
Pen
Wool felt/Nepal wool felt
Heavy, thick felt
Textile scissors
Pins
Bias tape
Sewing needle
Double embroidery floss
Decorative elements
Cotton thread
Puffy Paint

FELT FLOWER DECORATED SKIRT

MATERIALS:

Skirt or other garment
Parchment paper
Pen
Wool felt
Textile scissors
Sewing needle
Thread
Buttons

Embellishments made from wool felt are excellent for decorating any garment. You may want to use them to enhance the look of a lapel, a blouse, a sweater, a hat, a bag, or a solid-colored skirt.

First, choose your garment, such as the skirt shown here, and use pins to mark the area on your garment that you are going to decorate. Pick wool felt pieces in four harmonious colors. Cut out graphic flowers in different shapes and sizes. See pattern 24 on page 125.

Play with your design by stacking flowers in layers or one at a time, decorating flowers with buttons or other embellishments, mixing colors, or adding decorative stitches. When you are happy with your design and the flower constructions, sew the pieces together and attach them to your skirt.

DECORATIVE BELT WITH RIBBON TIES

This decorative belt is made with two layers of wool felt to give it some weight. Use the belt pattern 29 on page 134 to make the belt.

Using the patterns 29A and 29B on pages 133 and 134, cut out wool felt flowers and leaves. The yellow rosettes are made by cutting out the scalloped-edged circle that has a diameter of 2⅜ inches (6 cm) in wool felt, see pattern 29A on page 134. Cut the circle into a spiral shape. Start rolling at the center of the spiral, and roll outwards to make the flower shape. Put a little glue at the bottom of the yellow rose you just made, so that it does not come apart.

For the decorative elements, stack all "A" and "B" the flower shapes on top of each other, and stitch them together with a bead in the center. Attach all the flowers and star shapes to the dark, front side of the belt. Pin the two layers of felt for the belt together. Stitch them together with closely placed basting stitches. Firmly attach two ribbons, about 23¾ inches (60 cm) long each, to each end of the belt as you are stitching the belt pieces together.

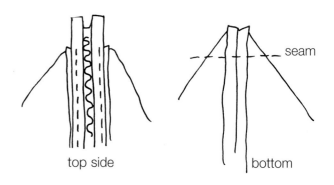

top side   bottom

seam

SPARKLY
MAKE-UP BAG

Cut out two pieces of wool felt measuring 7 x 5 inches (18 x 12.5 cm). (These dimensions include seam allowances.) Decorate the front of the make-up bag with wool felt circles that have a diameter of 2 inches (5 cm) and 1⅛ inches (3 cm) each. Attach the circles to the bag on top of each other with simple basting stitches. Felt a small ball from wool roving into the center of the circles. Make sure to slip a felting mat under your work when you are using a felting needle. Turn down a ⅜ inch (1 cm) wide fold along the whole length of the bag's long side on both felt pieces. Iron the fold on each piece of felt lightly with a damp cloth on top. Pin a zipper in place along the folded edges. The top of the zipper should be positioned against the fold on the felt's underside. Attach the zipper to the felt by either hand stitching or sewing on a sewing machine. After you have finished sewing the zipper in place, sew the bag's bottom and short sides together with the right sides facing each other. To give the bag a flat bottom, sew a short seam perpendicular to the bottom seam where the bottom and side seams meet. See the illustration on this page, and make the same seam on both corners of the bag. Cut off the triangular tips above the short seams. Turn the bag right side out. Finish off your make-up bag by attaching a tassel to the zipper ring.

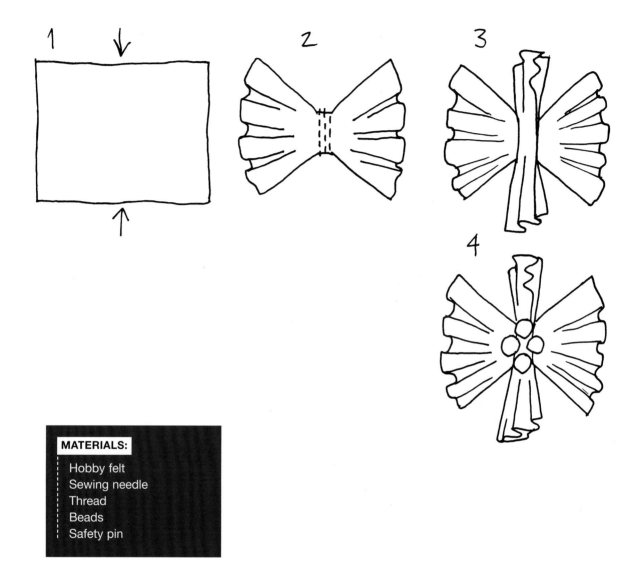

MATERIALS:

Hobby felt
Sewing needle
Thread
Beads
Safety pin

Who does not own a pair of shoes that could do with a little sprucing up? Just two pieces of hobby felt in different colors can give your shoes a extra, little something. Cut out two pieces of hobby felt measuring 2¾ x 5⅛ inches (7 x 13 cm) from each color (four total). Fold each piece of hobby felt into a bow shape, and sew it in the middle to fasten the shape. Choose one bow of each color. Place one bow perpendicular to and on top of the other bow. Stitch the bows together. Attach four, medium sized beads on the center of the double bow, and pin the decoration onto your shoe with a small safety pin. Repeat the process for the other shoe.

BRAIDED HEADBAND

To make this headband, you will need ribbons in different colors and of different materials. Select colors and materials that will look good together. Cut long, thin strips of wool felt to make "felt ribbons." To determine the length of the ribbons you must first measure the circumference of your head. Stretch the hair tie, and measure its length. Now take the measurement you got when you measured your head's circumference, subtract the length of the stretched hair tie, and add 1½ inches (4 cm) to get your final length. The extra 1½ inches (4 cm) of length will be used to attach the ribbons to the hair tie. If your ribbons are of different thicknesses, you can place two lengths of the same kind on top of each other to make the ribbons' thicknesses more equal. The model in the picture is wearing a headband made with a multicolored ribbon, one pink "felt ribbon", one purple ribbon with sequins, and one dark pink "felt ribbon." Select three lengths of ribbon. Fold the lengths around the hair tie, and sew them to the hair tie with a thin sewing thread. Braid the ribbons together. When you have braided the whole length, fold the remaining ends around the hair tie and sew them in place.

MATERIALS:

- Measuring tape
- Elastic band
- Sewing needle
- Thread
- Parchment paper
- Pen
- Nepal wool felt
- Hobby felt
- Textile scissors
- Decorative crowns
- Bells or beads
- Hobby glue

HEADBAND WITH PURPLE FLOWERS

Use a wide elastic band to make this headband. Measure your head's circumference, and cut the elastic band slightly stretched, to this measurement, plus a little extra length. Make a circle of the elastic band, overlap the ends, and fasten them with a needle and thread. Match the color of the thread to the color of the elastic band. Use Nepal wool felt and hobby felt to make the flowers. Cut out 5–6 petals. See pattern 41 on page 127. String the petals on a thread, pull on the thread to bunch the petals, and sew them together to make a flower. Next, fasten them on the elastic band.

Attach a colorful bell or large beads in the middle of each flower. I added a decorative crown to each flower, as shown on the head band in the picture. Sew the crowns on the flowers with a thread color that matches the color of the felt. If you do this, the stitches will not show. You can also attach the crowns to the flowers with hobby glue.

ANIMAL
HAIR CLIPS

MATERIALS

- Tracing paper
- Pen
- Wool felt
- Small, sharp scissors
- Hair clips
- Sewing needle
- Thread
- Embroidery floss
- Wool roving
- Plastic eyes
- Hobby glue

Draw your own animal faces, or use tracing paper to copy the images on this page and make these fun hair clips. To make the pig, cut out a piece of pink felt for the front and a piece of gray felt for the back of the face. Then cut out the glasses and a nose in felt. Attach the glasses to the pig's face, and embroider a frame around the glasses. Embroider the ears and a mouth on the pig's face. Put a little glue on a hair clip, and stick it between of the two layers of felt, from the side of the face. Sew some stitches into the clip and the felt to secure the clip in place. Both the cat's head and the frog's head have glued on plastic eyes and embroidered noses and mouths.

100%

Cut out squares of different colors in wool felt and hobby felt. Size the squares to fit on a square finger ring base. Make sure that your textile scissors are sharp, so that you get clean edges. Layer 3–4 pieces of felt on top of each other, and glue the layers together with textile glue. If you have a regular, round finger ring base, cut circles with an about ¾ inch (2 cm) diameter. Glue the felt stack together.

Place the felt stacks under pressure for a few hours until they have dried. Glue the felt stacks to the appropriately shaped finger ring bases. You may also want to experiment with making English licorice ear rings and cuff links.

MATERIALS:

Wool felt
Hobby felt
Finger ring bases
Textile glue/hobby glue
Textile scissors

Choose a more compact type of Nepal wool felt, and cut out a piece. The wool felt piece should be ⅜ inch (1 cm) wide and as long as the circumference of your finger.

Place the Nepal wool felt on a felting mat and felt on small pieces of wool roving. Use a thin felting needle for this work. The decorations can be varied. You may choose to felt a heart, letters, dots, or words on the strip of felt.

Sew the wool felt ends together on the back of your ring with a thread that has the same color as the felt. Try to make the seam invisible on both the outside and the inside of the ring.

You can make this super simple ring very quickly, and it is a perfect gift.

SUPER SIMPLE, SUPER CUTE RINGS

MATERIALS:

Nepal wool felt
Scissors
Wool roving
Thin felting needle
Felting mat
Sewing needle
Thread

MATERIALS:

Wool roving
Felting needles – medium
  and thin
Felting mat
Jewelry wire/eye pin
Darning needle
Hobby glue
Jewelry chain

You will need wool roving in three different colors for this project. Start by taking a piece of white wool roving. Place it on a felting mat, work it repeatedly with a felting needle (see page 7), and make it into a compact air balloon shape. Felt strips of red wool roving on to the shape with a thin felting needle. Wrap a little brown wool roving around the bottom of the shape, and attach it to the balloon using a thin felting needle. Shape a large loop on a short metal wire, or choose an eye pin with a large eye for the connection between the pendant and the chain. Make a hole into the top of the felted air balloon with a darning needle. Dip the metal wire or eye pin into glue, and insert it into the felted air balloon. Hang the air balloon on a chain. Stick a decorative pin into the bottom of the air balloon as an extra touch.

**AIR BALLOON
PENDANT**

MATERIALS:

Wool roving
Soapy water
Darning needle
Grill skewer
Jewelry chain
Wool felt/hobby felt
Hook and eye

**NECKLACE
WITH FELTED
WOOL BALLS**

Make the felted wool balls for this necklace by wet felting wool roving. Mix together about 1¾ cups (4 dl) of water and 1 tablespoon of soap. Choose seven equally sized pieces of wool roving and shape them into balls. Dip one wool roving ball at a time into the soapy water, squeeze out the water, and roll it between your hands. The wool roving ball will shrink as it is being felted. The wool will continue to felt as you roll the ball between your hands. After you have worked the wool for a while, dip the ball in cold water and then in warm water. Repeat this process a few times for each ball. Finish felting all the balls, and let them dry.

You may choose to decorate the felted balls with beads, embroidery floss, or felted wool yarn.

Before the felted balls are completely dry, pass a darning needle through them, and then thread the felted balls on a thin grill skewer.

Pull the felted balls off the skewer when they are completely dry. Thread a thin necklace chain through the holes in the felted balls, and place a thin, small, wool felt circle between each wool ball. Attach a hook and eye to the chain. You are now ready to wear your new necklace.

You can make a braided friendship bracelet by using several colors of wool felt or by simply using wool felt in only one of your favorite colors.

Choose wool felt in three different colors, and cut strips that are approximately ¼ x 13¾ inches (0.5 x 35 cm) in size. Place the ends at one side of the strips against each other, and sew them together. Braid the strips tightly. Sew the remaining ends together after you have finished braiding. Put a little glue on the ends, and slip them into ribbon crimp ends, one on each side of the braid. Attach a clasp to one ribbon crimp, and a ring to the other.

Give the bracelet away as a token of your friendship!

BRAIDED FRIENDSHIP BRACELET

This necklace brings back the sensibilities of times past. Start by finding a small, beautiful piece of lace. You may want to use antique lace with a nice shape. Place the piece of lace on top of some Nepal wool felt, and cut out the shape you want around the lace. When you have finished cutting out the shape, cut out the same shape again in hobby felt. The hobby felt piece will be the backing.

Sew the lace onto the Nepal felt with embroidery floss. Decorate the lace by sewing on some beads. Cut out some small leaves in wool felt and embroider them directly onto the Nepal felt using simple backstitches.

Sew the hobby felt onto the back of the Nepal felt. Use small basting stitches, and a thread of the same color as the felt to sew the two pieces together. Make one hole on each side of the felt where you would like your chain to attach. You can use a large tapestry needle to make the holes. Embellish and strengthen the holes by embroidering a star pattern around each hole with embroidery floss. Thread a ring into each hole. Attach a necklace chain to these rings. Make another hole in the felt at the bottom center of the piece. Embroider a star pattern around this hole as well, and attach a ring. Place a freshwater pearl on a pearl bail pin and attach it to the ring.

NECKLACE WITH LACE

MATERIALS:

A piece of lace
Textile scissors
Nepal wool felt
Hobby felt
Sewing needle
Embroidery floss
Thread
Beads
Wool felt
Tapestry needle
Jewelry rings
Necklace chain
Pearl bail pin
Freshwater pearl

APPLE TREE BROOCH

You can use the pattern on this page to make this charming apple tree brooch. Copy the pattern onto tracing paper, and transfer the image onto a piece of Nepal wool felt. When you have finished cutting out the apple tree shape in Nepal wool felt, cut out the same image in hobby felt. The hobby felt piece is for backing. Choose wool felts in different colors and cut out ten round shapes for the apples. Attach nine of the apples to the tree with a simple cross stitch.

Next place the hobby felt tree under the Nepal wool felt tree, and sew the pieces together with blanket stitches, keeping in mind that one of the apples will "hang down from the tree." Start sewing around the tree, when you get to the spot where the apple will be hanging, extend your thread about ¼ inch (0.5 cm) from the tree. Attach the apple to the thread by sewing blanket stitches around the apple with the same thread. Stop at the same spot where you started sewing on the apple. Sew buttonhole stitches around the hanging apple's thread up to the tree. Continue sewing the blanket stitches around the tree. Finish off by sewing a brooch pin on to the back side of the apple

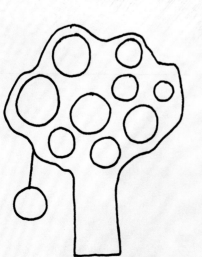

MATERIALS:

Tracing paper
Pen
Nepal wool felt
Wool felt/hobby felt
Small scissors
Sewing needle
Embroidery floss
Brooch pin

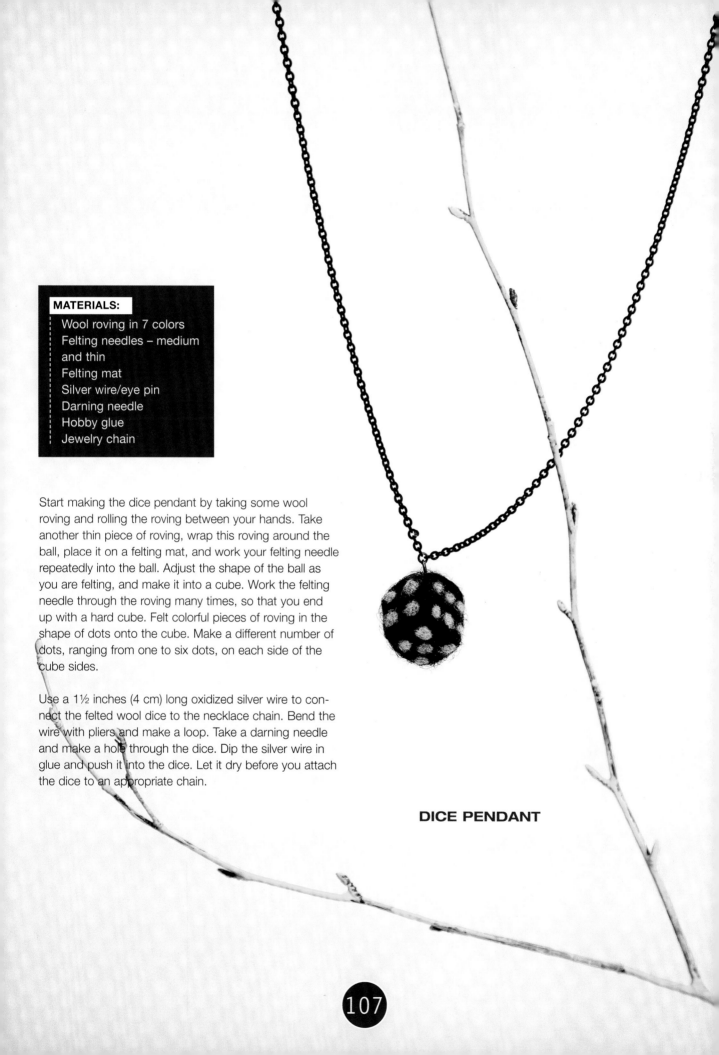

Start making the dice pendant by taking some wool roving and rolling the roving between your hands. Take another thin piece of roving, wrap this roving around the ball, place it on a felting mat, and work your felting needle repeatedly into the ball. Adjust the shape of the ball as you are felting, and make it into a cube. Work the felting needle through the roving many times, so that you end up with a hard cube. Felt colorful pieces of roving in the shape of dots onto the cube. Make a different number of dots, ranging from one to six dots, on each side of the cube sides.

Use a 1½ inches (4 cm) long oxidized silver wire to connect the felted wool dice to the necklace chain. Bend the wire with pliers and make a loop. Take a darning needle and make a hole through the dice. Dip the silver wire in glue and push it into the dice. Let it dry before you attach the dice to an appropriate chain.

DICE PENDANT

107

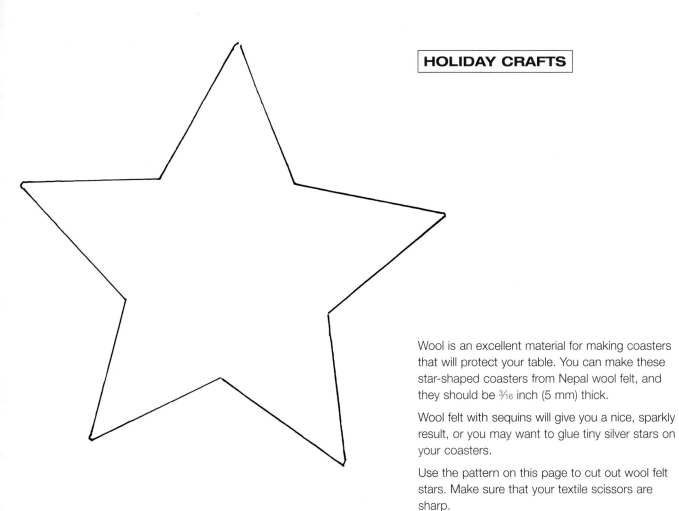

Wool is an excellent material for making coasters that will protect your table. You can make these star-shaped coasters from Nepal wool felt, and they should be ³⁄₁₆ inch (5 mm) thick.

Wool felt with sequins will give you a nice, sparkly result, or you may want to glue tiny silver stars on your coasters.

Use the pattern on this page to cut out wool felt stars. Make sure that your textile scissors are sharp.

Pour some silver glitter onto a plate. Brush textile or hobby glue around the star's edges and dip the star into the glitter. Let the star dry for a while before you slip it into a plastic bag, and put it under pressure until it is completely dry.

STAR-SHAPED COASTERS

MATERIALS:

Tracing paper
Pen
Wool felt with sequins/
 Nepal wool felt
Textile scissors
Glitter
Hobby glue/textile glue
Plastic bag

STAR-SHAPED
GARLANDS

MATERIALS:

Tracing paper
Pen
Wool felt/Nepal wool felt
Textile scissors
Hobby glue
Glitter
Sequins
Thin fishing line
Sewing needle
Plastic bag
Prisms

To make a template for this mobile's stars, you can use a cookie cutter or the star drawing on this page.

Start by transferring the star shape onto wool felt. Cut out as many stars as you will need for the entire mobile. We used five fishing lines with five stars on each line, so we cut out 25 stars.

Use both wool felt and the thicker Nepal wool felt for your stars. After you have finished cutting out the stars, glue on some sequins and glitter to decorate them. Let them dry for a while before you slip them into a plastic bag. Place the plastic bag with the stars under pressure. You may want to use some heavy books for this.

Thread a thin fishing line onto a needle. Attach a prism at one end of the line to weigh it down. Use the needle and pull the fishing line through the center of each star. Make a loop at the end of the fishing line when you have finished attaching the stars. This loop should be large enough for a curtain rod to pass through it.

To store the mobile, wrap the lines around a piece of cardboard, and tape the ends of the lines to the cardboard.

What is more traditional during the holidays than white wool hearts with red decorations? You can make endless variations of these simple hearts by just changing up the decorative elements. Using the pattern on this page cut out two hearts, place wool roving in between the pieces, and sew the heart pieces together with either basting stitchs or blanket stitchs.

When you are done decorating the hearts, you can hang them on your Christmas tree, on a cupboard, in a window, or on some shelves to create a festive holiday atmosphere.

Embellishments:

- Sew blanket stitches with black embroidery floss around the heart. String seed beads on a needle and thread, and sew a word in the middle of the heart.

- Attach a large, decorative button in the middle of the heart. Sew blanket stitches around the heart.

- Attach red seed beads around the heart with a ⅜ inch (1 cm) space between the beads, and write a word on the heart with tightly spaced beads.

- Sew blanket stitches with a double sewing thread around the heart. Fasten a piece of lace in the middle of the heart.

- String red seed beads on a thread, and sew them on the heart. Fasten the thread after every five beads as you work your way around the heart. Attach old ribbons with initials and buttons to the heart.

- Glue red sequin stars all over the heart.

- Attach tiny seed beads all over the heart. Use a very fine sewing needle and white thread to attach the beads.

HOLIDAY HEARTS

BOTTLES WITH ANGEL WINGS

MATERIALS:

Empty, clear bottles with
  screw caps
Wool felt/Nepal wool felt
Textile scissors
Sewing machine
Sewing needle
Thread
Sequin stars/circles
Hobby glue
Plastic bag
Metal wires 8⅝ inches
  (22 cm) long each
Pliers
Nippers
Translucent paper
Pins

You can make felt angels by covering clear bottles, about 8⅝ inches (22 cm) high, with wool felt or felted wool from a garment.

Fasten the wool felt around a bottle with the wrong side out, pin tightly, and trim to size. Remove the wool felt from the bottle and sew, wrong side out, either on a sewing machine or by hand.

Turn the wool inside out and pull it over the bottle.

Cut out angel wings for the felt covered bottle using the same wool felt or thicker Nepal wool felt. See pattern 47 on page 122.

Use hobby glue to decorate the wings by gluing on sequins and glitter. Allow the wings to dry for a while before you put them in plastic bags. Place heavy books on the wings and let them dry completely under pressure. When they are dry, you can sew the wings onto the bottle. Use a basting stitch to attach the wings, so that when Christmas is over, you can easily remove the wings from the bottle. Store the wings separately so that they will preserve their shape for the next time you use them.

To complete your angel, make a halo using a 8⅝ inches (22 cm) long metal wire about approximately a 16 gauge jewelry wire, (about 1 mm thick). Bend the wire in the shape of the halo depicted on this page (see the drawing). Use pliers to shape the halo and nippers to cut the wire. Place the lower part of the halo between the threads on the bottle's neck. Shape the top so that it looks like a "floating" halo.

The smallest angel in the picture has wings made from thick, translucent paper. The wings are fastened to the wool felt with pins.

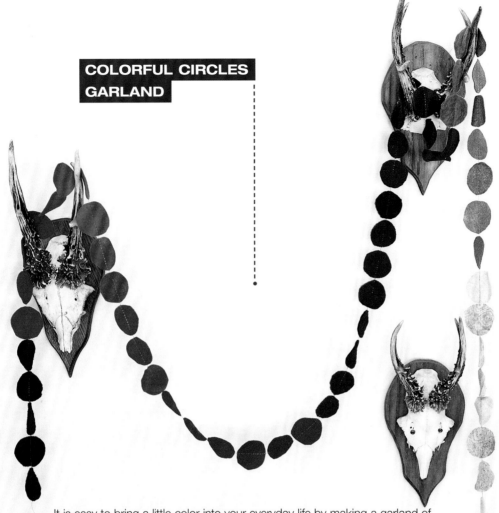

COLORFUL CIRCLES GARLAND

It is easy to bring a little color into your everyday life by making a garland of differently colored shapes, and there are so many places where this colorful garland will fit in. Try hanging one by a window, around a door opening, draped on a wall, or just let it lie as it falls on a table.

Start your project by deciding on a shape that is easily reproduced in large quantities. We used circles, which are easy to make. Make a paper circle template with about 1½ inches (4 cm) in diameter, place the template on pieces of wool felt, and cut out several circles at a time. You may want to make all your circles of the same color or choose a range of colors, such as the colors of the rainbow. When you have cut out all the circles you want to use, place them in a row. Choose a large, straight stitch setting on your sewing machine and sew straight through all the circles, one after the other. Make sure that you have a length of thread about 8 inches (20 cm) long before you start sewing the first circle, and leave about 8 inches (20 cm) of thread after the last circle. You can make several circle garlands at a time and drape them all around each other.

MATERIALS:
Paper
Pen
Wool felt/hobby felt/felted
  wool garment
Textile scissors
Sewing machine
Sewing thread

Tip: When you want to store your garland, wrap the garland around a piece of cardboard so that the string does not become entangled.

SWEET HEARTS

Cut out two hearts from wool felt. See pattern 22 on page 123. Pin a gathered tulle ribbon all around and between the two heart pieces. Place some fiberfill between the hearts and sew them together. String seed beads on a needle and thread, and fasten the beads around the heart.

MATERIALS:

Tracing paper
Pen
Wool felt/Nepal wool felt
Textile scissors
Gathered tulle ribbon
Pins
Fiberfill
Sewing needle
Thread
Seed beads

CREDITS:

Principal photography by Erika Lidén except where noted.

Step-by-step photography by Tone Rørseth, pages 20, 29, 35, 58, 59, 68, 83, 94, 95 og 112

Styling and Illustrations by Tone Rørseth

Designer: Lise Mosveen

about the author:

Tone Rørseth is a jewelry and accessories designer, as well as a photo stylist for various interior design magazines. Tone graduated from the Beckmans School of Design in Stockholm, Sweden.

PATTERNS

The patterns are drawn to fit this book's pages. All are 100% unless otherwise noted. Some patterns will need to be enlarged on a photo copier.

Felt Envelope
p. 36

PATTERN 2

UP

85% of actual size; enlarge by 115%

Flower Garland w/ lights
p. 60

PATTERN
20 ×

FOLD

PATTERN
47

Bottle w/ Angel Wings
p. 115

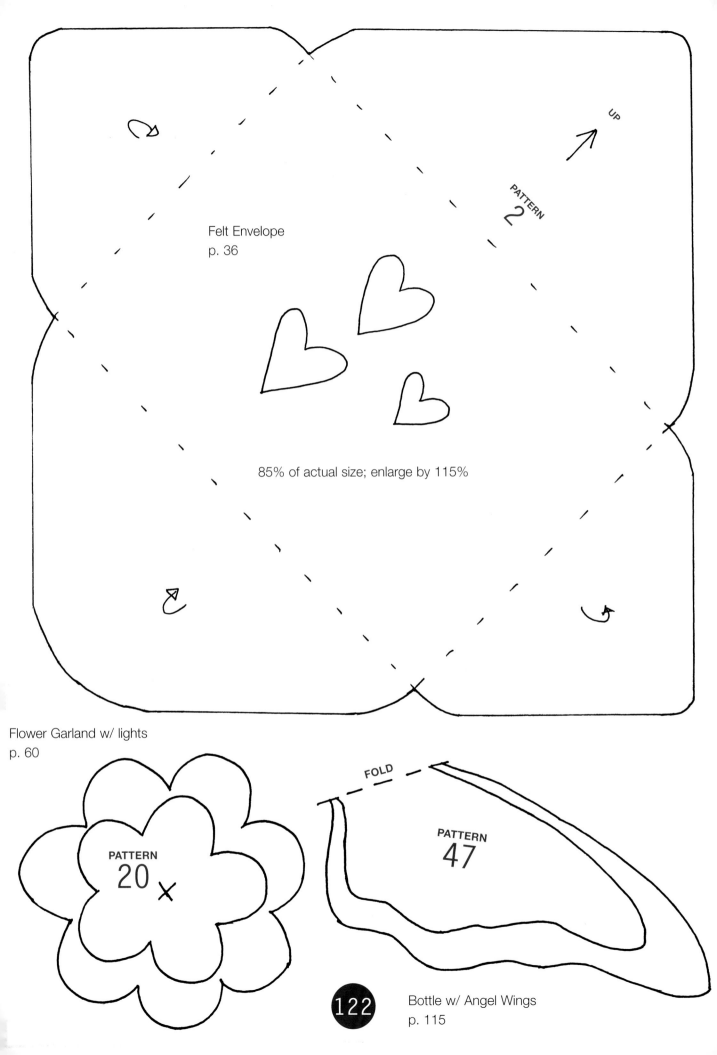

Heart
p. 64

Sweet Hearts
p. 117

PATTERN
22

Laptop Cover
Embellisment
p. 42

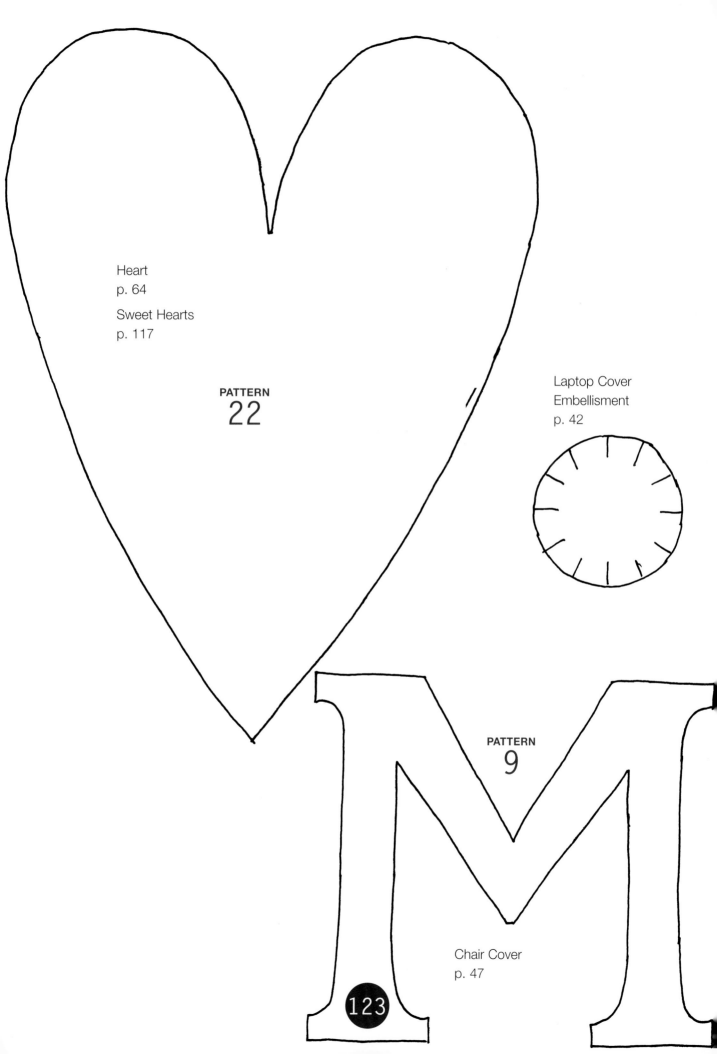

PATTERN
9

Chair Cover
p. 47

Refrigerator Letter
Magnets
p. 36

90% of actual size;
enlarge by 110%

Felt Flower Decorated
Skirt Decorations
p. 89

x2

PATTERN
7

Love Diary
with Bookmark
p. 40

ME & Y

PATTERN
7

PATTERN
7

126

Fun Hats for Kids
p. 83

PATTERN
26

95% of actual size;
enlarge by 105%

fill dotted section of
the top of the hat with
wool roving

FILL

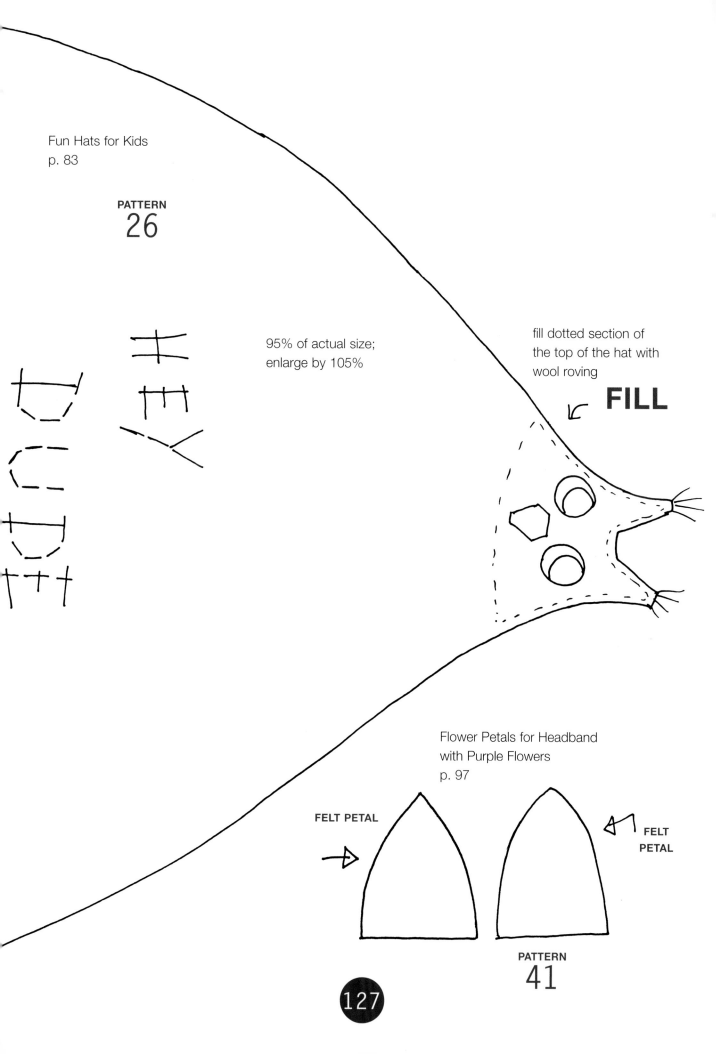

Flower Petals for Headband
with Purple Flowers
p. 97

FELT PETAL

**FELT
PETAL**

PATTERN
41

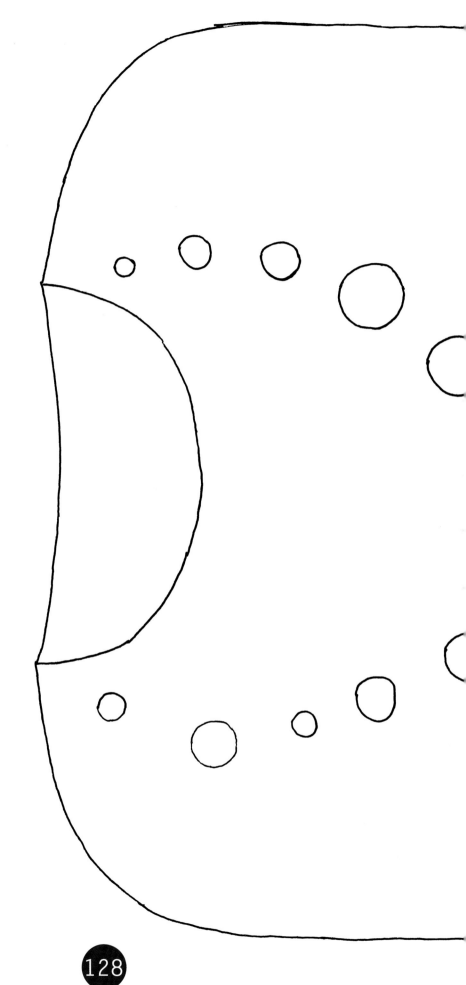

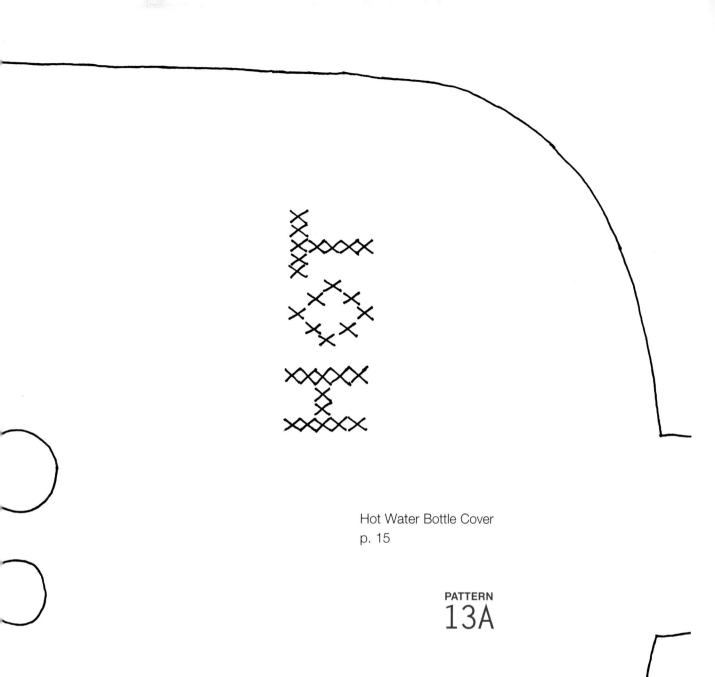

Hot Water Bottle Cover
p. 15

PATTERN
13A

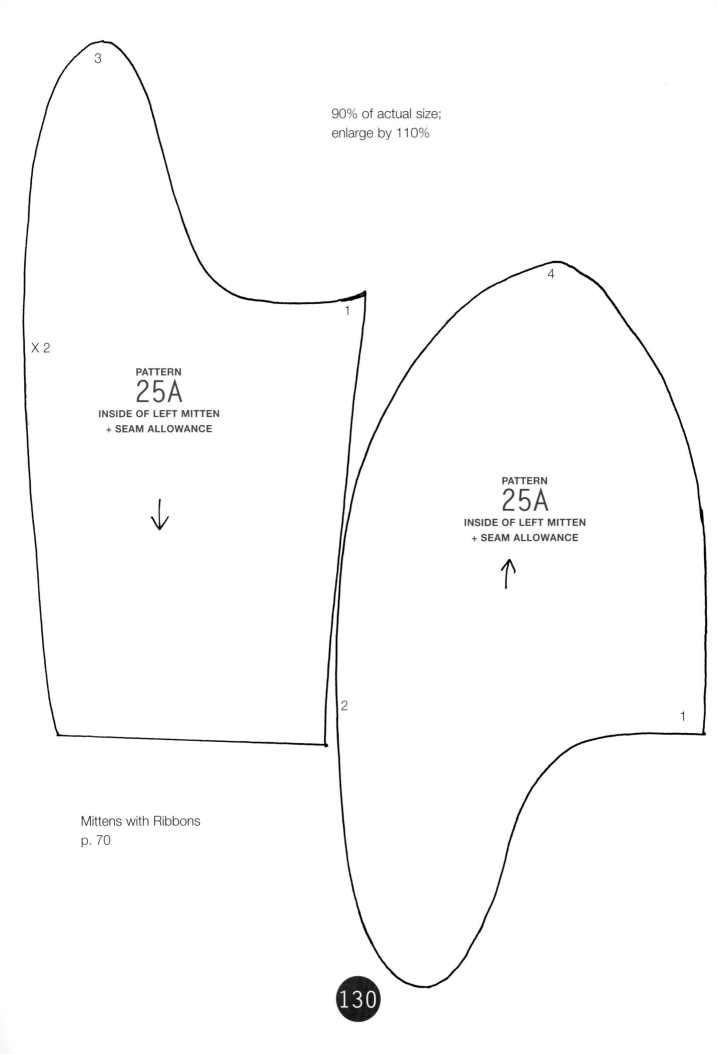

90% of actual size;
enlarge by 110%

3

X 2

PATTERN
25A
INSIDE OF LEFT MITTEN
+ SEAM ALLOWANCE

↓

1

2

4

PATTERN
25A
INSIDE OF LEFT MITTEN
+ SEAM ALLOWANCE

↑

1

Mittens with Ribbons
p. 70

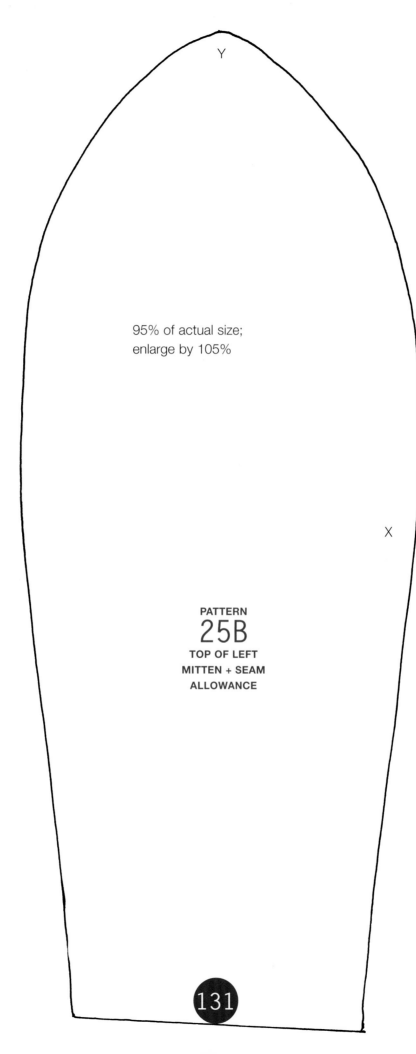

Y

95% of actual size;
enlarge by 105%

X

PATTERN
25B
TOP OF LEFT
MITTEN + SEAM
ALLOWANCE

131

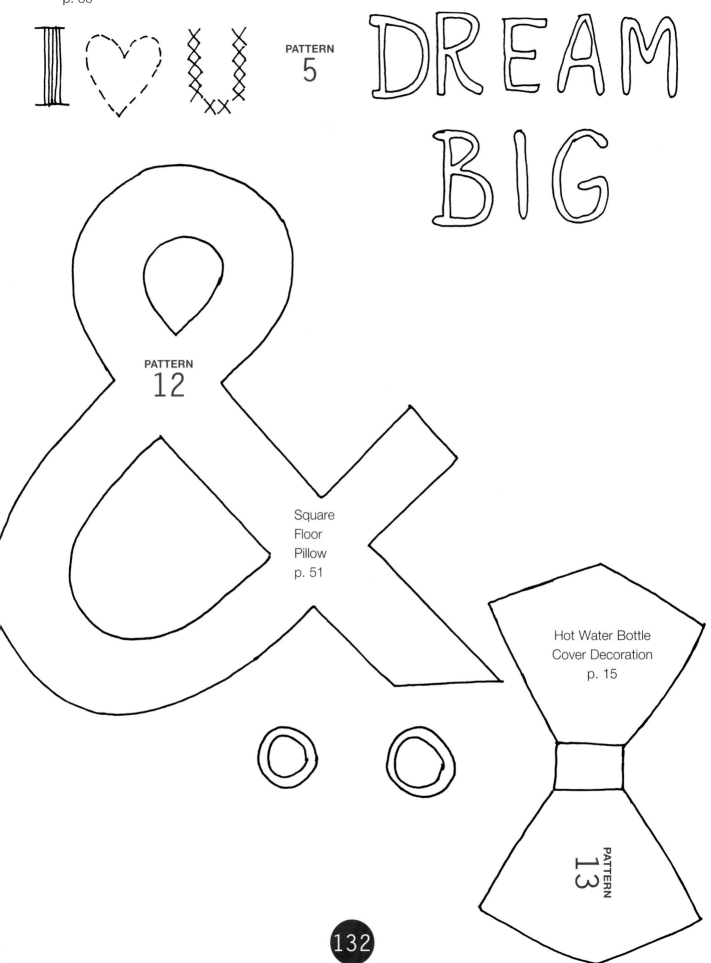

I ♥ U

PATTERN
5

DREAM BIG

PATTERN
12

Square
Floor
Pillow
p. 51

Hot Water Bottle
Cover Decoration
p. 15

PATTERN
13

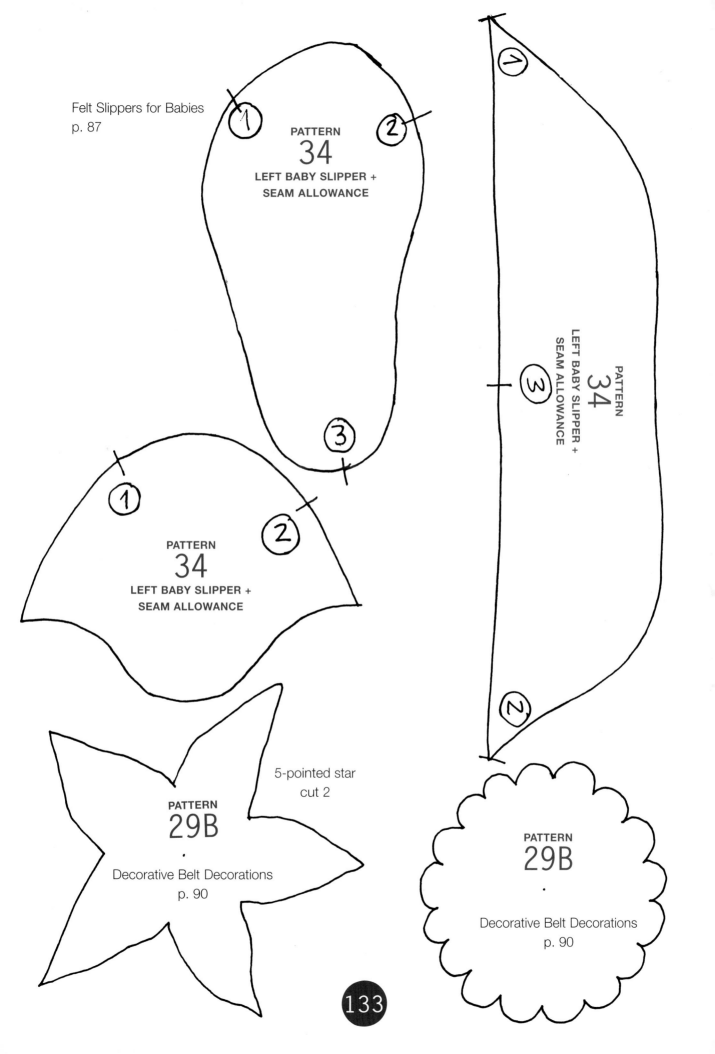

Felt Slippers for Babies
p. 87

PATTERN
34
LEFT BABY SLIPPER +
SEAM ALLOWANCE

PATTERN
34
LEFT BABY SLIPPER +
SEAM ALLOWANCE

PATTERN
34
LEFT BABY SLIPPER +
SEAM ALLOWANCE

PATTERN
29B

5-pointed star
cut 2

Decorative Belt Decorations
p. 90

PATTERN
29B

Decorative Belt Decorations
p. 90

133

CENTER
cut on fold

Belt is 90% of actual
size; enlarge by 110%.

BELT PATTERN
29

Decorative Belt
with Ribbon Ties
p. 90

PATTERN
29A

PATTERN
29A

PATTERN
29A

PATTERN
29A

PATTERN
29A

Use this as pattern to
make rosette.

PATTERN
11
Luggage Tag
p. 41

FRONT

BACK

HOME

85% of actual size;
enlarge by 115%

PATTERN
5

Embroidery Hoop Art
p. 30

PATTERN
5

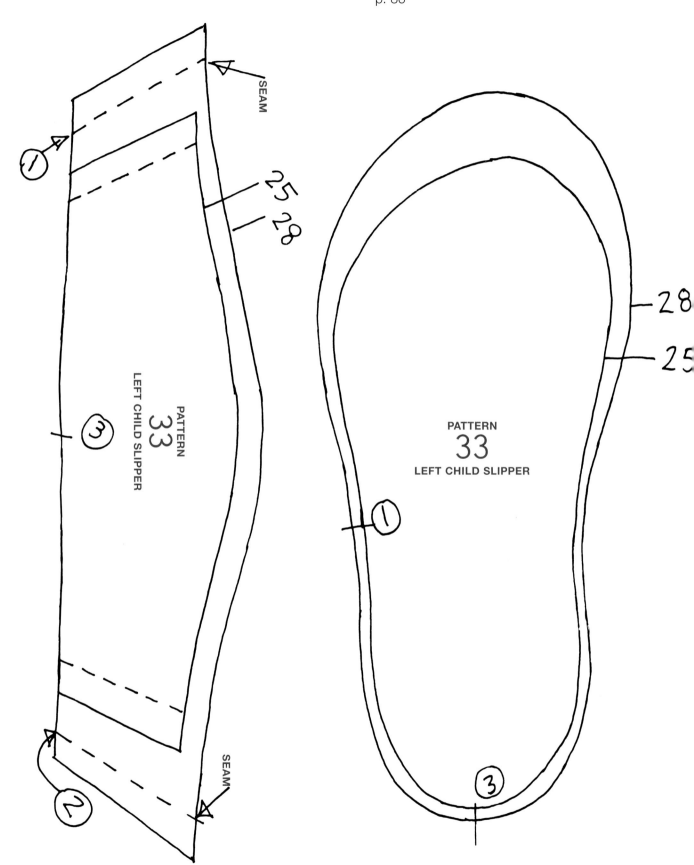

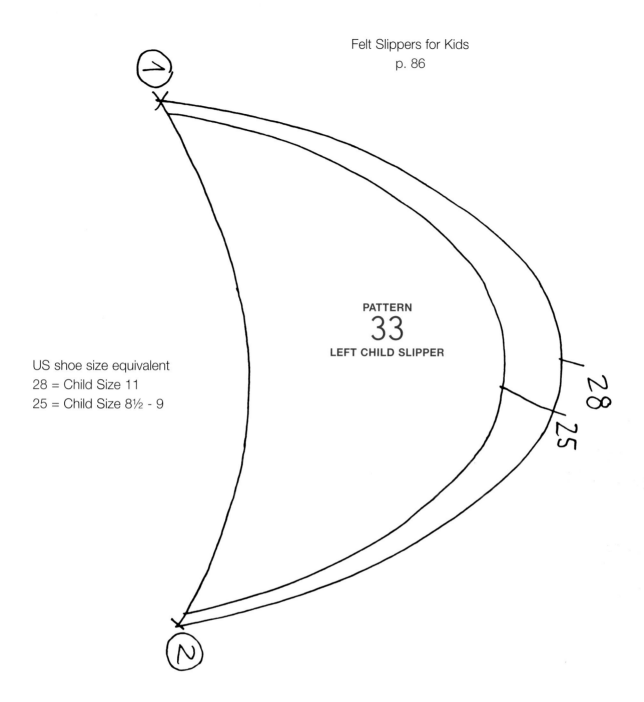

PATTERN
33
LEFT CHILD SLIPPER

US shoe size equivalent
28 = Child Size 11
25 = Child Size 8½ - 9

Cut two of each pattern; one
for the left slipper, one for
the right slipper

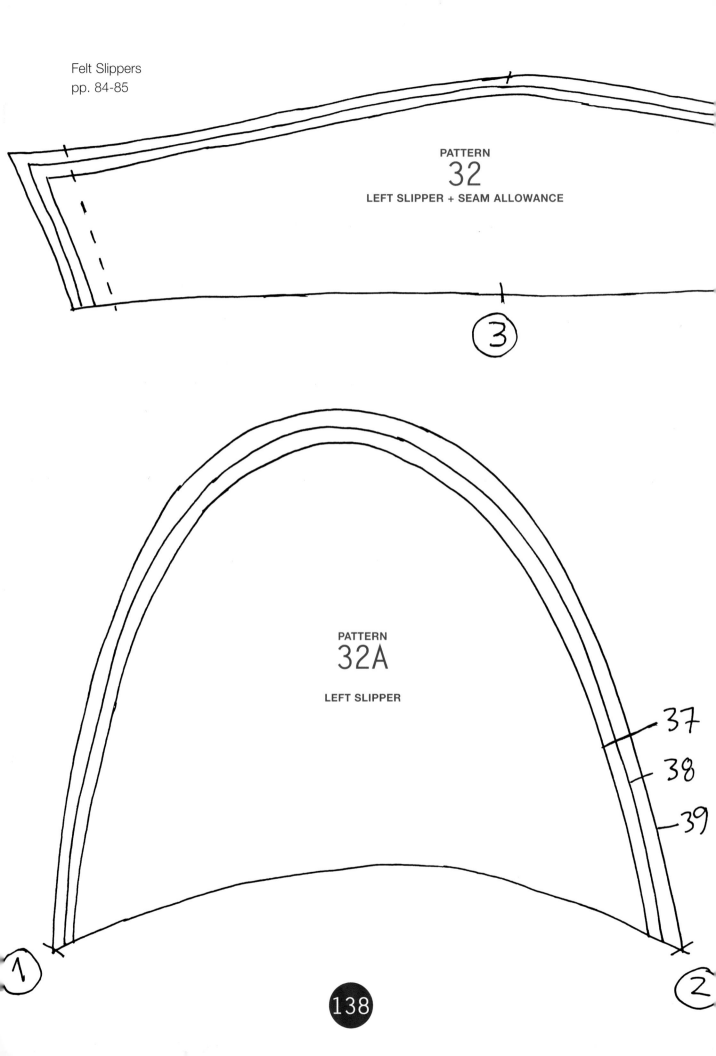

Felt Slippers
pp. 84-85

PATTERN
32
LEFT SLIPPER + SEAM ALLOWANCE

③

PATTERN
32A

LEFT SLIPPER

37
38
39

①
②

Felt Slippers
pp. 84-85

39

38

37

PATTERN
32
LEFT SLIPPER + SEAM ALLOWANCE

39

38

37

US shoe size equivalent
37 = 6 1/2
38 = 7 1/2
39 = 8 1/2

①

②

Cut two of each pattern; one
for the left slipper, one for
the right slipper

139

③

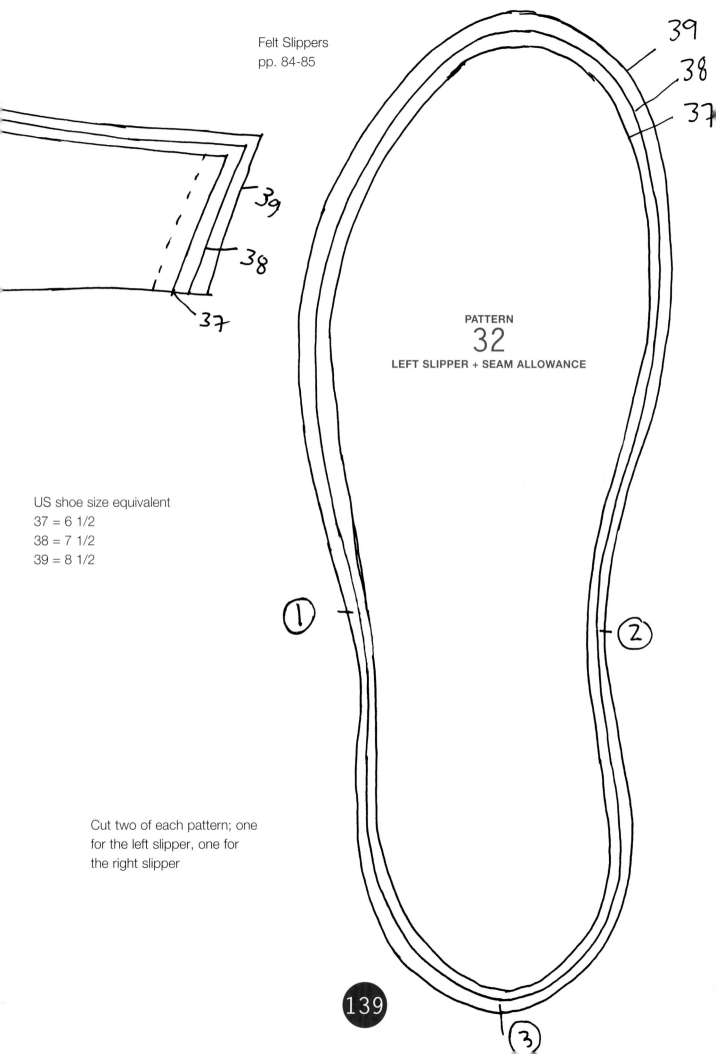

ACKNOWLEDGMENT & THANKS

This book would not have been so richly filled with ideas without the inspiration and help that I have received:

Many thanks to my fantastic and extremely gifted photographer, Erika. I am very grateful for the patience my husband and children have shown me. Thanks to Linda and Anette for inspiration and proofreading. To Malin and Anna for assisting with the photography. To Carina and Marie for props.

To my mother-in-law for lending me her house, watching the children, and her nimble fingers.

Thank you to my beautiful models: Elisabeth, Linnea, Love, Fanny, Vincent, and Bianca Louise.

To Mom Anne for sewing help. To Panduro Hobby for wool. To Intrade and Boråstapeter for wallpaper.

INDEX